Praise fo

'Unambiguously brilliant. Jude Jennison's visionary approach to building teams is brought to life through the spirit of Opus in this bold and compelling book. The OPUS Method is rooted in and inspired by her years of equine experiences with senior leadership teams. It provides a practical guide to leadership as a human endeavour which puts relationships and reflection at the heart of effective team performance.'

Adrian Packer CBE, CEO, Core Education Trust

'Never has a book or approach been more pertinent to how we consider the impact and opportunity for our behaviours to make a difference to our lives. Jude beautifully highlights the impact of dissonance, and the opportunity for this to drive curiosity to find enlightened alignment to team success.'

Alex Arundale, Chief People Officer, Advanced

'Jude Jennison has written a masterpiece. This book is a must read for anyone wanting to develop their leadership skills, knowledge, and potential. At the heart of it all, we need to know who we are and how we bring ourselves into relationships. This book helps you to discover that within the context of organizations and teamwork. Beautiful, moving, and succinct, *Opus* offers leaders a framework for leadership that will be a game changer. Simply outstanding.'

Dr Veronica Lac, Executive Director, The HERD Institute®

'Whether you've spent a little or a lifetime leading teams, this book will help you reflect on your behaviours and how they help (or hinder!) in driving team performance. Each chapter made me pause for thought, and consider what I need to maintain, or do differently, to be a better leader. Opus may not be with us anymore, but his wisdom lives on in Jude, in her incredible talent for coaching leaders, and in this book.'

Kristy Rowlett MHRA, Head of People Development,
Wesleyan Assurance

'Jude's insightful, clear and very wise guide to leading brilliant teams, gives simple, effective and practical advice to leaders of all levels. I think we should be thanking Opus, Jude's horse, who clearly massively influenced the content of this lovely book. The clearly laid out steps, combined with the wonderful examples of her horses showing us how it's done (or not done!), bring each chapter to life in a relatable, heart-warming and authentic way. I'll be buying this for my team.'

Jess Lonsdale, Internal Communications Director, Virgin Media

'The study of teams is not new, but teamwork is more important than ever. Jude's thoughtful and useful work explores the roots of effective teams though OPUS: Organization (leadership roles), Pillars (relationships), Understanding (information), and Stories (governance). Mastering and applying her 12 team dynamics will enable teams to fulfil their potential for impact.'

Dave Ulrich, Rensis Likert Professor, Ross School of Business,
University of Michigan Partner, The RBL Group

'In *Opus*, Jude Jennison brilliantly shows the path of mastery to develop true authentic top team leadership by revealing the invisible, the unspoken and the intangible with the help of her own top team of horses. Full of stories that make the intangible tangible, Jude shares a holistic team development process that guarantees deep shifts and sustainable results. A must-read for every top team ready to grow together.'

Nicole Heimann, Founder & Co-CEO
Heimann Cvetkovic & Partners

'Working with Jude, her colleagues and her amazing team of horses has been truly transformational at all levels of our company. The incredible step change in understanding across our leadership team, which is described in the pages of this book, acted as a catalyst, creating the foundations for our COVID-19 recovery and future growth.'

Peter Marsden, Director and Co-Founder, Entec Si

'While reading, I kept thinking of a phrase: "Horses are ego killers". Ego has no chance of survival in a herd. Each individual is important. I would never want to compare the socialization of a herd of horses with that of a company. That would be banal and superficial. But deep inside both organizations, you find basic commonalities of togetherness and survival. These are the "hidden dynamics." In this book, Jude Jennison penetrates them and makes them visible.'

Gerhard Jes Krebs, HorseDream Founder and EAHAE President

'Leadership is changing. Immeasurably. Future leadership is shifting from "me" to "we" and in this book, Jude Jennison brilliantly captures how next generation leaders will need to show up in this transforming world. It's so refreshing to have a leadership book crafted from the experiential, the grounded reality and the real world, from someone who has walked the precarious corporate and entrepreneurship road.'

Will Murtha, Leadership, Mindset & High-Performance Coach,
Transformational Leadership Coaching

'Through the OPUS Method Jude has articulated an invaluable methodology that is accessible to all those who are committed to truly leading great teams. By bringing into sharp focus those dynamics that often go unspoken in teams, Jude has set out an invaluable guide for leaders who strive for the best for themselves and others. I consider this an essential read for those looking to create highly functioning teams in an ever-evolving world.'

Amardeep Gill, Partner, Trowers & Hamlins LLP

'An insightful book, that brings to life Jude's approach to what I would call a much more 'human' leadership than we normally see. Whether you are a leader or not I would recommend this book and approach, it will help you crack how to influence those around you.'

Andy Scrase, Head of HR Content, Telefonica UK Limited

'*Opus* is so much more than a book about team dynamics. It could seriously result in a significant improvement in both relationships and performance, for you and your teams. It is a combination of the author's wisdom and experience, interwoven with stories and practical workbooks, which significantly extend the learning process. Stories reveal examples of our human frailty, with the simplicity, and clarity of reality, provided by our equine friends.

Highly insightful, impactful, practical, and useful. *Opus* is written in a compelling writing style which draws you in from the beginning. This is a book about improving the relational element of teams, resulting in happier people, and improved performance.'

Gina Lodge, CEO, The Academy of Executive Coaching

OPUS

THE HIDDEN DYNAMICS
OF TEAM PERFORMANCE

JUDE JENNISON

First published in Great Britain by Practical Inspiration Publishing, 2021

ISBN   9781788602600 (print)
        9781788602594 (epub)
        9781788602587 (mobi)

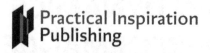

For Opus,
the master of non-verbal communication,
your presence lives on in all of us whose lives you touched.

We come together as strangers,
Willing to surrender
To the vulnerability of relationship.

We embrace uncertainty
And breathe into possibilities,
Working in harmony, as one.

Together we change the world,
And in so doing,
We ourselves are changed.

Jude Jennison, New Year's Day, 2021

CONTENTS

FOREWORD

I have worked with Jude for about eight years. My role has changed from CEO sounding board and business advisor to stable hand, yard manager, horse handler at workshops, her caterer and argumentative friend. During this time, I have listened to Jude saying that the horses respond and pick up on our energy and react to it immediately. At times Jude has claimed they can feel it from across a 10-acre field. Having ridden for 50 years, I have sometimes felt this was stretching the truth a little – until, that is, I read that one sentence. All of a sudden, I got it.

That hidden feeling, that sixth sense we ignore, the prickles on the back of your neck, the instinct to look behind you in the dark, that feeling of awe when the headmaster stepped into the room, or the safety and warmth when I stepped through the front door of my grandmother's house as a child. Hidden, non-verbal, real, authentic feelings that I felt deep in my bones. I didn't argue with them and certainly never ignored them; they were there always and in an instant. Regrettably, as we get older and certainly within business we forget or shut down these feelings and eventually we become unaware of them being part of us.

Learning with Jude and her equine team and then reading this book is like looking into a verbal mirror that enabled me to re-connect with that subliminal awareness within me. Awareness of self that made me smile and cringe at the same time, awareness of others I have worked with in a team that made me proud and a bit embarrassed, and awareness of the environment I work in now that makes me realise how the macro and micro worlds around me help me to tune in to that sixth sense to the benefit of what I am trying to achieve.

Jude's words of wisdom – derived from years of hard commercial experience coupled with ten years of reflection, learning and observations of horses and humans – shine gently, openly and succinctly through her book, powerfully enough to make you stop, think and smile inwardly at your own habits, behaviours and stories.

If you are brave enough to be honest with yourself and bring your authenticity to your own life and the teams you work with, then the concepts and ideas in this book can help your team deliver results greater than the sum of the parts. You can achieve results that you and your team never thought possible.

How do I know? Simple: I have witnessed it in action on scores of occasions with those six beautiful horses walking side by side with strangers, gently showing the way, guiding and talking to us with hidden words and instructions to navigate dangers and obstacles as a team in perfect harmony, and I've witnessed the joy, power and satisfaction of the team when they have done it.

Alan Sheppard, COO, BSweet UK Ltd

PROLOGUE

Opus is Latin for 'work' and is a term commonly used in music. When you lead a team, you orchestrate a work of art. You lead a team to execute performance.

Opus was also a thoroughbred horse who lived in my care for seven years. Born in Australia, he also lived in New Zealand and Bahrain before coming to the UK. Due to an early injury, he never raced but he had an extensive riding career with his owner Laura.

The day I met Opus, he was standing calmly outside a stable with Laura. I was looking for my second horse so I could expand my Equine Facilitated Leadership business and work with teams. Recruiting a member for your team is critical. Balancing skills, experience and personality in a team can create harmony or discord. It requires everyone to shift a little and work together as one.

After six months of drama with my first horse Kalle (rhymes with Sally), my confidence was at rock bottom. After being face down in the mud with concussion because Kalle had headbutted me, and electrocuted when she sniffed the electric fence, causing her to rear up and leave me terrified, I needed a calm, confident horse. Opus gave me confidence, but not in the way I'd hoped or expected.

Aged 24, he was calm, gentle and kind. The day Opus walked onto my yard, he looked me up and down and decided I wasn't up to the job. He took charge. In my desire to be a compassionate leader and feed off his confidence, he took advantage of me. Every time I led him, he dictated the pace. Sometimes he went really slowly, and I struggled to get him to pick up the pace. Other times, he jogged ahead, and I struggled to get him to slow down.

Every day was a power struggle. When Kalle spooked, as she often did, I had to breathe deeply and stay calm for her to relax into. When I did this with Opus, he took charge even more. He was never afraid like Kalle; his high energy was not fear but the desire to be in charge. I needed to step up to him. One day as he was leading me to the field, he was pushing and shoving and spinning round. I stopped and said: 'Stop it. Walk properly.' To my utter surprise, he did. Opus taught me how to balance compassion with power, clarity with curiosity, confidence with sensitivity. He taught me the knife-edge of leadership where the masculine and feminine energies are in complete harmony.

I called Opus the MD because nothing happened on my yard without his approval. When I led Kalle and Opus together, one of them would walk fast and one would walk slowly. Whilst Kalle required me to keep my energy low and calm, Opus required me to raise my energy and match him in his power. It was a delicate balance to keep the team together.

As I expanded my equine team over the years, Opus integrated every new horse into the team. Each time, the new horse would spend a week or two with Opus before being turned out in the whole herd. Opus called the shots. His communication was clear, never ambiguous. If you stood up to him, you could easily enter a power struggle. I saw many senior leaders do that with him. Opus never gave in. He seemed to know how to handle different clients and give them what they needed. With MDs and senior leaders, he would put them in their place, kindly but firmly. There was no room for ambiguity. With graduates and young leaders, he was gentle, willing and kind and did everything they asked so they grew in confidence.

This is Opus. This is the work of teams. This is how it is to lead a team of different personalities: some requiring compassion in the form of gentleness and calm; others requiring power and strength without dominance.

Opus was a work of art and he orchestrated my team for seven years. He taught me to continually fine-tune my leadership and lead my team with curiosity, understanding and kindness as well as clarity, power and strength. The energy of his leadership and teamwork lives on in all of those whose lives he touched.

INTRODUCTION

One of the questions leaders ask me most is: how do I get people to do what I need them to do? I think this is the wrong question. That question implies that you have all the answers and if you can get everyone to do what you want, then you'll have brilliant teamwork. It's not that simple.

This book encourages you to explore a different question: Who do *I* need to be to work effectively in a team? And: who do *we* as a team need to *be* to do great work?

If you shift your focus from *I* to *we* and the *doing* to the *being* of teamwork, you'll discover the hidden dynamics of team performance. This book focuses on those dynamics – the non-verbal communication that occurs constantly in a team, often unconsciously.

The hidden dynamics are often unspoken. They require the team to stretch, to develop greater transparency, openness and honesty. It's vulnerable so it's easier to keep them hidden. Except it isn't because those dynamics aren't hidden at all. They play out unconsciously in your team, day in, day out. They erode trust, damage relationships and cause division, so differences of opinion continue and teams waste time and energy pushing through. It's exhausting.

The complexity and fluidity of teamwork cannot be under-estimated, but they usually are. Continuous improvement in leadership and team behaviour needs time, awareness and effective communication.

Just like an athlete or a sports team, a high-performing team in business doesn't happen by accident. It takes continual effort to ensure that everyone is clear on their role, takes responsibility and accountability for success, repeatedly raises their game, works cohesively in the team, resolves differences of opinion without ego, and balances results and relationships.

Welcome to *OPUS: The Hidden Dynamics of Team Performance*. In this book, I outline the four steps and 12 hidden dynamics of the OPUS Method that can be used to develop your team and improve performance. It specifically explores the unconscious patterns of behaviour that sabotage teamwork and provides an opportunity to communicate more openly and effectively as a team.

Who is this book for?

I've written this book specifically for senior leadership teams, but it could equally be applicable to any team. You can even apply the methodology with your family. My previous books focused on who you need to be as a leader. *Leading Through Uncertainty* explored the impact of disruptive change (Jennison, 2018) and *Leadership Beyond Measure* covered critical leadership traits such as courage, compassion, trust and respect (Jennison, 2015).

This book explores how you work together as a team. Most senior leadership teams are made up of brilliant individuals, but it's the relationships between individuals that make or break the team, and therefore determine how successful that team and business are. I've written this book as a practical and reflective guide for senior teams to work through together to find the essence of team performance.

I've assumed that as a senior leadership team, you have a clear strategy, vision and values. If not, I recommend you explore these in detail in parallel. Subtle nuances of leadership and communication fundamentally change the way a team works together.

Real and lasting change happens when you feel your leadership and witness the shift in each other. You can develop as individuals in isolation, but success in business requires leaders and teams to be lifelong learners together, so you adapt your behaviour to meet the needs of the team.

Most senior teams are skilled in discussing business strategies and resolving problems. This book focuses on the non-verbal behaviours which are often unconscious and influence the quality of the relationships and therefore the alignment of the team.

Unconscious patterns of behaviour are ingrained from an early age as we respond to childhood situations and then repeat those same patterns of behaviour throughout our lives. Unless you become conscious of those behaviours, it is almost impossible to create behavioural change.

How to use this book

This book is designed to reveal the hidden dynamics of team performance. It is designed to provoke reflection and conversation in your team. The book starts with a section called 'Ground Zero', where I set out the context of developing team performance, the impact of uncertainty on teamwork and provide an overview of the OPUS Method. Steps One to Four explore the crucial non-verbal behaviours of the OPUS Method that every team needs to be aware of and often isn't, because they are usually hidden.

Each chapter begins with an illustrative case study of a client who has worked with me and my horses. In many cases, clients have written these stories themselves so you will read the story of what happened, what they learned and how they applied it to their own teamwork later on. This book is not about the horses though. The chapters are inspired by working with them, for the benefit of applying the learning to your team.

At the end of each chapter, I recommend you reflect individually and then share your responses with your team and agree an action plan to develop the team based on what you have learned.

 Download the *OPUS Method of Team Performance* workbook from www.judejennison.com/opus and record your reflections and actions.

My inspiration for the book

Most of the non-verbal behaviours that form the hidden dynamics of team performance outlined in this book are based on over a decade of working with thousands of leaders and teams in an equine facilitated leadership setting. This is an embodied form of leadership that involves working with a herd of horses to provide a learning experience for clients to develop their leadership and teamwork skills.

Horses respond based on your non-verbal communication, which includes your energy, emotions, thought processes, assumptions and intentions and much more. Most of the chapters in this book have been inspired by learning with horses. Horses pick up on the subtle nuances of what you are thinking and feeling, and respond in a relational way to you and your team. 'You literally feel your leadership,' explained one HR Director.

Horses require clarity of direction, a strong relationship based on trust and mutual respect, and the choice to follow through free will, rather than because they have to. They come with you when you balance the result with the relationship in harmony. They plant their feet and refuse to engage if either of these is missing. Their desire to be safe means they always work as a team or herd, and they work in an inclusive way, embracing differences of opinion whilst staying focused on being together in unison.

Why me and why this book?

Prior to running a leadership and team development company, I spent 17 years working for IBM and led UK, European and global teams, including running a budget of $1 billion, which I reduced by 25% over two years. I've worked in teams where I felt the joy of connection and effective communication, in teams where I felt disconnected and under pressure with no let-up and in one team where I was micro-managed to the point where I felt I couldn't breathe. I now work with leaders and teams who want to challenge the status quo and work cohesively together to do great work in the world.

I am devoted to my work and always have been. I am inspired and motivated by working in brilliant teams with brilliant people, overcoming challenges together and finding new ways of living and working in harmony. My hope is that by working through this book, you find the joy and love for your work and for your team.

I believe strongly that work can be joyful and life-enhancing; I believe that business has a major impact on the world and if we are to create the radical change that is needed in society and for our planet, we need to find the joy in it. I am working to create a world of work that works for everyone and for everyone to have deeply fulfilling work that makes a difference. I hope you will join me in creating your own fulfilling teamwork. It matters.

Ground Zero
LAYING THE
FOUNDATIONS

In which we explore the impact of uncertainty and introduce the OPUS Method...

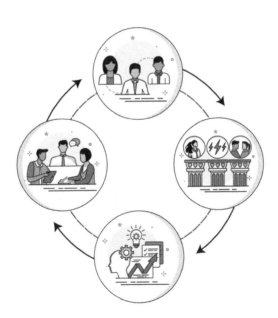

Chapter 1

DEVELOPING THE TEAM

In which we set the context for outstanding team performance...

Inspiring teamwork

Imagine a team who leap out of bed every morning, excited about the day and the week ahead. Imagine that same team committing to each other, communicating openly, defining the priorities, and letting go of the things that are not business critical. Imagine the transparency of communication, the quality of conversation, and the honesty around how you feel and what you think, without friction, tension and frustration.

Imagine the effortless flow, without pushing through. Imagine the clarity of direction, the desire to execute together, and the accountability and commitment to each other, as well as to the business. Feel the energy of your team in flow – inspired, energised and enthusiastic. Teamwork is important. Intellectually we all know that. But when you actually feel the flow of effortless teamwork in your body, you know you're on the right path.

Most of the books and training for leadership and teamwork focus on action and doing. Build the vision, define the strategy, define roles and responsibilities, articulate the company values and culture and off you go. In reality, it is far more complex to lead a team, especially through change.

The real shift happens when you focus on who you are *being*, in addition to what you are doing. Relationships and results. Reflection and action. These are the hidden dynamics of teamwork that are outlined in this book.

In this book, I take a closer look at the non-verbal behaviours that enable teams to work cohesively together. The OPUS Method of Team Performance outlines four steps that reveal 12 hidden dynamics of a team and provide insights into how you can work with them to enhance team performance.

A McKinsey report (Banholzer, 2019) on high-performing innovation teams highlighted that whilst most leadership development is focused on the individuals in an organisation, 'reframing the discussion from individuals to teams helps tremendously to unlock performance'.

My work has led me to explore human existence and behaviour, to understand who we are being in the doing, and specifically, who everyone in the team is being and the relationships amongst that team.

Tangible, cohesive teamwork

People spend so much time in their heads working out what to do next, what to think, what to say, even how to behave. They have learned to suppress emotions and to switch off the wisdom of the body. This numbing stops people from showing up authentically.

This needs to change. The unconscious patterns of team behaviour sabotage your ability to work cohesively and adapt quickly. The OPUS Method uncovers those hidden dynamics, revealing the unspoken thoughts, feelings and energy that unconsciously impact the team. It provides a methodology for your team to explore what is happening under the surface and replace misunderstandings with clarity and stronger relationships.

If businesses want to solve the world's problems, and I hope they do, we need more than sitting in a white box in an office with sterile furniture and a whiteboard to write on. We need more than transactional interaction on the end of Zoom or Microsoft Teams or any other kind of virtual technology.

We need leadership and teamwork that is so tangible and palpable that we feel it and know that change is inevitable. We need a deeper level of connection: for the sake of mental well-being, the benefit of humanity and making a difference in the world.

The dichotomy and paradox of cohesive teamwork is that you never really know how to do it until you're doing it. You know when you're in flow; you know when it's awkward and clunky, and often teamwork does feel awkward and clunky. The tension of competing objectives, the challenges of difficult conversations (either embraced or avoided), the elephant in the room, the not wanting to rock the boat.

I always encourage teams to be polarised. I know that sounds crazy. But if you all think the same and act the same, you'll get groupthink. There can be no creativity or innovation without a spark, without an ability to build on each other's ideas. And that requires you to think in different ways, behave in different ways, and to even have different values, beliefs, experience and skills. And therein lies the magic. The challenge of team performance is in the blend of everyone and everything. In pure harmony.

Psychological safety

In order to align as a team, everyone needs to flex their behaviour, and you need to feel psychologically safe to do so, together. Team psychological safety is a shared belief in the team that it is safe to take risks and that the team can count on each other for support, without blame, judgement or criticism. It is crucial for teams to be open and honest in their communication and to foster a culture of learning, rather than one of punishment and shame. This has a huge impact on stress and wellbeing in the team, as well as performance.

Psychological safety enables teams to have honest conversations, openly discuss issues and work through them together. Team members need to feel safe to take a risk, knowing that they can regard mistakes and errors as part of the learning process, instead of being punished or ridiculed. This is essential in times of change and uncertainty because innovation and creativity are needed to move forward and create opportunities from adversity and chaos.

If teams do not feel psychologically safe, people will withhold information, not ask for help and not offer support to each other. A lack of psychological safety can lead to shame, ridicule and judgement and creates divides and tension in the team.

Psychological safety encourages a culture of learning, which enables teams to continually refine how they do things. If a team leader sets the tone that it is not safe to make mistakes, innovation cannot occur, and the team will not discuss issues openly. This leads to discussions happening behind people's backs and increases blame, judgement and criticism.

The team must feel safe to challenge each other without feeling threatened and to see each other as human beings who are all trying to do their best work. By replacing blame with curiosity, teams enhance their understanding of each other, support each other more collaboratively and encourage continual learning together.

Willingness to change

Team performance requires everyone to continually modify their behaviour and work in service of the whole. Most people want to change other people but not themselves. Team performance only happens when everyone is willing to change and reveal the hidden dynamics that are derailing the team.

Throughout your career, you've honed your skills in your job, but what about the inter-dependencies within the team? Many teams are a group of leaders who are individually brilliant at what they do. Some may even refer to themselves as high-performing because individually they are achieving results. What makes a brilliant team is the development of the relationships within the team. The ability to pull together against the odds, to collaborate so effectively that you over-achieve and deliver things that were not even within sight.

If you focus solely on developing the individuals in the team and don't make the effort to develop the relationships, the team will never perform at its optimum. If you don't set the team up for success, or you create a toxic or unsafe environment, the team can't be courageous. They will be afraid to take risks for fear of failure. This prevents learning and growth, innovation and creativity, all of which are critical to the success of teams and business.

Working with teams, I've discovered that their attitude and commitment to reinventing themselves and the willingness to learn are fundamental to change. Unless you are willing to change your own behaviour and can support everyone in doing the same, nothing will change, and the team will continue to under-perform or rush around fire-fighting issues and struggling to manage their high workload.

Changing team behaviour

We often call leadership, teamwork and communication 'soft skills'. Certainly, they are less tangible and much more difficult to measure than technical skills. But there is nothing soft about the hard work that is required to align a team, to work through your differences, to be inclusive, to ensure everyone plays their part, to respond to changing priorities and iron out miscommunication issues.

People tell me that changing someone else's behaviour is hard. I'd say it's almost impossible. But you can change your own. Look there first. What can you do differently to invoke change? Changing behaviour means exploring what is working and what is not. It requires conversation, vulnerability, the willingness to consider a better way of doing things. A desire to do what is right in service of the whole team, rather than self-serving. Yes, it's hard. As you learn and change your behaviour, those around you change theirs too, so the team is always in a state of flux, requiring adaptability and awareness. This is the premise of the OPUS Method – to reveal the hidden behaviours, understand them and work with them to align together as a team.

It's uncomfortable being vulnerable in a team. It's uncomfortable to accept that there might be a better way of doing things and that sometimes you might be the spanner in the works without realising it. Not because you intended to be, but because you might be the one who is out of alignment. Or you may be the one who holds a different perspective that is needed in the team to prevent groupthink.

It may appear easier to do what you've always done. It's often more comfortable to carry on as before. And you know how that ends. Unresolved differences of opinion. Frustration. Tension in the team.

When one person changes their behaviour, everyone responds differently and so the team is changed. Therefore, it is beneficial for teams to explore their development together, so they adapt together in a more conscious and supportive way.

Changing behaviour is challenging because it requires you to accept that there is a different way of doing things, to let go of the old behaviour and practise the new. Change creates uncertainty so teams often avoid it and opt for the status quo, even though it derails them.

The OPUS Method provides a step-by-step methodology to reveal the hidden dynamics of your team's behaviour. It has been designed to be adopted step by step, each step building on the previous one, however, you could also pick any one of the 12 dynamics and work through it with your team and it will improve your teamwork, communication and understanding of each other. Take as long as you need to include the changes, embed them in your teamwork before moving on to the next step. All change creates uncertainty and personal change requires a foundation of psychological safety which you will further enhance by increasing clarity, improving relationships and reducing ambiguity and misunderstandings in the team.

Chapter 2

TEAMWORK IN UNCERTAINTY

In which we understand the impact of uncertainty on teams...

How do I lead?

These are some of the questions that clients ask me when they walk through my gate, literally into a field of uncertainty, for a day of learning with horses.
  'How do I lead?'
  'How fast do I walk?'
  'Do I lead from the front or the side?'
  'How do I build a relationship (with the horse)?'
  'How do I hold the lead rope?'

> *They sometimes later admit that they also ask themselves the following questions internally:*
> *'Will I look an idiot in front of my team?'*
> *'Will the horse come with me?'*
> *'Will I be the only person who can't get a horse to engage with me?'*
> *'Can I lead?'*
> *'Will I be found out?'*
> *'Am I about to be publicly humiliated?'*
> *Whilst often unspoken, these are hidden dynamics that impact the way people show up.*

Change and uncertainty

The *Oxford English Dictionary* describes uncertainty as the 'state of being uncertain' and 'not known, reliable or definite'. Whenever there is change, there is uncertainty as you carve a new path. Uncertainty is imposed upon us by external events – economics, politics, social and environmental change, new rules and regulations.

In addition, you also create uncertainty when you evoke change in your life or work. When you change your job, get married, have children, or even book a holiday, you create uncertainty. If you've ever agonised over being stuck in traffic when you have a plane to catch or wondered if the hotel you've booked will be ok and the kids will enjoy the expensive holiday, you'll have experienced the impact of uncertainty! The feeling of being out of control; the discomfort of not knowing the outcome.

Learning also creates uncertainty as you explore new ways of doing things. This is essential in teams to be able to continually flex to meet the changing needs of the team, business or situation. Existential psychologist Bugental (1990) explores the continual process of learning as a leap into the uncertainty of life itself:

'Being alive is a full-time, lifelong job for which we are all poorly prepared, about which we continually have to learn, and in which repeatedly we have to make changes as we go' (p. 36). Life, by its very nature, is uncertain, and the uncertainty of learning means that teams often avoid it.

Our brains naturally look for certainty because it makes us feel safe. In uncertainty, you have some of the information but there are always bits of information missing. Like a jigsaw puzzle with missing pieces, your brain will fill the gaps and make up what it believes the picture to be. You fill those gaps based on your personal preferences, previous experience, skills, thoughts, values and beliefs. Since everyone has different experiences, everyone will have a slightly different view of the world in uncertainty. That's why politics causes such a heated debate because everyone has different views that shape their beliefs.

The challenge with uncertainty is that once you make a decision, you act as though it is true and will look for additional information to justify your decision. Once you have come to a conclusion, it's difficult to change your mind, so you may dismiss new information as it arises and hold steadfast to the initial decision. As a team, in uncertainty, you will naturally have different views on how to handle it and how to lead through it, and this can lead to debates and polarised views.

Teams need enormous flexibility and a willingness to have your mind changed through team discussions. This is a learned behaviour and takes time. By recognising this as a team, you engage in a better quality of conversation if you have the maturity to have your mind changed by the opinions of others. You will rarely have group consensus so someone will always have to give.

The zone of uncertainty

Uncertainty is uncomfortable. We feel safe within the known state of the comfort zone. It's tried and tested. Uncertainty requires us to step into a place of not knowing, where nothing is a given. It creates self-doubt if you focus on what is not known or guaranteed, instead of remembering what is known and understood. Every leader I work with can lead. They do it every day in their normal place of work, but as soon as they leave their comfort zone and enter a new and unfamiliar environment, the uncertainty and self-doubt kick in.

Figure 1 shows a continuum of how comfortable we feel from a state of being bored on the left, through the state of feeling comfortable, to feeling stretched and into overwhelm on the right. Throughout the day, according to what you are doing, you move along this continuum from one end to the other.

Figure 1: The zone of uncertainty

Most people spend the majority of the time in the comfort zone. This is the realm of the things you know how to do. If you spend too much time in the comfort zone, life and work start to become dull and you are likely to move left in the picture towards a state of boredom. These are tasks that are not interesting and therefore don't stimulate you. A handful of these tasks is acceptable if the rest of your time you feel stimulated, but if your day is full of boring tasks, you will quickly lose interest. Too much time in a state of boredom leads to apathy and even depression.

If you step out of your comfort zone and do things that stretch you, you have an opportunity to learn and this is where leadership happens. You make decisions without all of the information. You may provide clarity for others in uncertainty as a result of your leadership. Leaders and teams therefore need to feel confident to move from the known of the comfort zone into the uncertainty of leadership.

You can see in Figure 1 that leadership is out of the comfort zone because leadership happens in those moments where you need to take a stance, make a decision and influence others, without necessarily having all of the information to do so. Relationships with others also create uncertainty as you have no control over how the rest of the team will respond. You can influence but not control. Children are used to being out of their comfort zone and continually learning. As adults, there is often a tendency to shut learning down because it is uncertain and uncomfortable. The ability to continually learn and flex is crucial as a team.

However, if you experience too much uncertainty at one time or have to do too many new activities, you might find you move into a state of overwhelm. When people hit overwhelm, they respond in different ways. Some people shut down and refuse to engage with the uncertainty or change. They will typically justify their decision and say they are not afraid to change but 'don't want to'.

This is a way of shutting down and then avoiding overwhelm and fear. Some people respond to uncertainty by being disruptive and looking for all the arguments as to why something is wrong. This is also a state of overwhelm although the emotion is often suppressed, and it may be an unconscious response.

Often when someone in a team is disruptive or resistant, the rest of the team try to drag them along, try to persuade them that they need to take action. If someone in your team is being disruptive or resistant, dragging them further into overwhelm will not help. It will be met with more resistance and disruption. Once someone is in overwhelm, you can either give them space to process it in their own time or you can provide support to bring them back into a state of leadership and learning. You ignore and negate their emotion if you persuade them that they don't need to be overwhelmed. This is not helpful or healthy.

Whenever there is uncertainty, teams automatically look to the leader of the team for clarity, even if there is none. The desire for certainty and clarity is a normal response to uncertainty. Margaret Wheatley said: 'Every situation is what it is, sometimes lovely, sometimes difficult. Every situation is workable. We're fully in the river. Learning how to keep our heads above the water' (Wheatley, 2010, p. 133).

There is a need to embrace the uncertainty of life and work, to be ok with the discomfort of not knowing and trust that we can be creative in uncertainty and see it as an opportunity for change. By its very nature, uncertainty means you don't have all the information, so be prepared to say so and be honest about what you do and don't know as this will develop trust.

A balance between comfort zone and leadership is healthy for most teams. Too much uncertainty pushes the team into over-whelm whereas not enough change leads to boredom. Teams need to work together and support each other in uncertainty, sharing honestly how they feel about the uncertainty, pulling together to create opportunities from perceived adversity.

It's a continual state of fine-tuning, and of course everyone in the team will have a different experience of this too. Some people love being out of their comfort zone and prefer to spend more time in their leadership zone, whereas others will prefer to operate in the comfort zone and need to be encouraged not to become too static.

Awareness of where you and the team are, individually and collectively, is crucial to be able to keep the team moving forward together in a way that doesn't cause anyone to switch off or burn out. The hidden dynamics outlined in this book will help you and your team reveal information that supports you as you stretch out into the zone of uncertainty.

An existential crisis

Existential psychologist Irvin D. Yalom (1980) outlines four existential givens that govern the way we interact with the world – death (including the end of something as we know it), freedom, isolation and meaninglessness. Yalom argues that existential anxiety increases as we become more aware of these givens.

When the Covid-19 pandemic hit in 2020, we experienced a heightened awareness of all four existential givens as we lost our lives as we knew them (as well as loved ones), our freedom was curbed with lockdown rules, people felt isolated working from home, and many started to question the meaning and purpose of their work and life.

No wonder then that the world was plunged into a heightened state of anxiety as people grappled with the chaos, confusion and polarisation that occur in uncertainty. Uncertainty invokes an existential crisis, and this has an impact on teams as everyone has a different experience.

As you develop greater self-awareness, you increase awareness of the existential givens which can also invoke the anxiety of uncertainty. Being a lifelong learner is increasingly recognised as a crucial skill for leaders, yet it can create an existential crisis of confidence. Many leaders are afraid to engage in learning and this is especially common in senior teams who may not want to be vulnerable in front of their colleagues.

The stakes of learning are high; the rewards are higher. Leaders and teams therefore need support in the form of coaching or mentoring as they develop self-awareness, make sense of their existence and achieve their potentiality without being derailed by the anxiety invoked by the uncertainty of the existential givens.

Hofmann (2014) explains how emotion helps us make sense of our existence: 'In the frenetic pursuit of creating certainty, we lose the grand mystery of being.' All emotions have value to help us transform how we experience life (and work). Uncertainty invokes strong emotions, and it is important to move through those emotions and not to suppress them. In my book *Leading Through Uncertainty* (Jennison, 2018), I delve deeper into uncertainty, the emotional responses we have and how to navigate them.

How uncertainty affects the team

Uncertainty has a major emotional impact on everyone in different ways. Some respond by only focusing on the positives. Others feel dragged into the depths of despair but may try to put a brave face on it because they think they should. Suppressed emotions are part of the hidden dynamics of team performance. If emotions remain suppressed and it is not ok to talk about negative experiences in your team, those emotions will have a negative impact in the long term.

Dialogue is essential at times of uncertainty to give people space to make sense of how the uncertainty impacts them and to use the support of the team to help everyone stay connected and move forward. You don't have to agree when you are polarised in opinions, but it helps to understand each other's point of view. There is a tendency to create distance when you don't agree and spend more time with those you agree with. Instead, see emotion as an opportunity to deepen relationships and seek to understand through dialogue and listening.

Uncertainty creates an existential crisis out of which a team can pull together, support each other and look for opportunities, to grow both individually and collectively, as well as practical opportunities to do things in a different way.

Margaret Wheatley (2017, p. 226) explains that 'Life changes through emergence.' She argues that our desire for certainty causes us to resist the uncertainty of emergence and to repeat habitual patterns of behaviour, even though they are not working. 'Opening to the uncertainty, to the need for a new way of seeing, is not what we humans do well. We use our big brains and our powers of cognition to resist change' (Wheatley, 2017, p. 196).

There is no certainty in the emergence of life. Let go of control. It is a myth. Instead, the quality of your relationships and leadership skills will equip you to handle the uncertainty of life and work. This book explores some of the hidden dynamics of a team and I encourage you to be open in your continual exploration of how you and your team behave in the uncertainty of change – either in your business or your team.

Chapter 3

THE OPUS METHOD OF TEAM PERFORMANCE

In which we introduce the four steps of the OPUS Method of Team Performance...

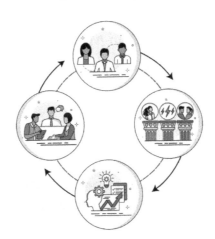

Four steps to team performance

In this book, I set out the 'being' of teamwork, focusing specifically on non-verbal communication. The non-verbal communication drives much of leadership and team behaviour, often unconsciously. Eugene T. Gendlin (2003, p. 33) explains the challenge of exploring non-verbal behaviour: 'Since a felt sense doesn't communicate itself in words, it isn't easy to describe in words'.

Nevertheless, this book sets out (yes, in words!) the OPUS Method, examining how the hidden dynamics of non-verbal behaviour impact your team and how you can lead and communicate more consciously. The OPUS Method consists of four steps and 12 hidden dynamics:

1. The **Or**ganisation Model: three team roles to align your team.
2. The **Pi**llars of Vitality: three cornerstones that underpin vitality in the team.
3. The **U**nderstanding Approach: three team perspectives to inform decision-making and action in uncertainty.
4. The **S**tories Blueprint: three stories that people unconsciously believe to be true that create division or cohesion.

Step 1: The Organisation Model

Most teams are made up of a group of individuals, all with individual targets and objectives. It's incredibly difficult to get everyone moving together at the same time, at the same pace and in the same direction towards the same vision and goals. When the Chief Finance Officer considers their role to be fundamentally different from the role of the Chief People Officer, and the Sales Director is not aligned with the Operations Director, you can see why teams engage in lengthy debates over competing priorities.

One of the most common things I hear is that people don't have time to… Don't have time to build relationships, don't have time to ask people how they are, don't have time to take a break, be creative, get clear on the strategy, align, etc. But if you do what you've always done, you'll get what you've always got and that leads to ineffective and unproductive use of time, something most teams experience on a regular basis. It's exhausting as well as frustrating.

We all have a tendency to default to a particular style of leadership, but different styles are useful for different reasons, with different people and in different situations. The ability to flex between the styles enables you to get the best out of your team. In Step 1: The Organisation Model, there are three key roles that are needed in every team:

1. **Leading from the front** – to provide clarity and direction.
2. **Leading from the middle** – to execute, coach and support.
3. **Leading from the back** – to hold the team accountable and make sure things stay on track.

Chapters 4 to 6 explore these roles in more detail, identifying the primary responsibilities of each role in the team, as well as the pitfalls to watch out for. Many companies still operate a top-down hierarchy. The Organisation Model is designed to work with both a flat organisation and a top-down hierarchy. In reality, a combination of the two is required for effective teamwork. If you rely solely on hierarchy, decision-making is only done at the top. The team will wait to be told what to do and won't take responsibility.

If the organisation is flat and completely democratic, it often results in chaos, anarchy and stasis because teams rarely agree on every point. Constant debate occurs until everyone gets bored and switches off, creating distance in the team. Someone has to take a stance, make a decision and provide clarity of direction, but it doesn't always have to be the same person.

The Organisation Model combines the need for decisiveness and collaboration. Team performance happens when everyone in the team has the flexibility to move into an appropriate position according to what is needed in any given moment. When all three roles of leading from the front, middle and back are balanced and in harmony, the team builds momentum and moves forward faster together.

Step 2: The Pillars of Vitality

Most organisations are operating at high speed. Results are paramount and people are exhausted. Everything is critical, and everything is a priority. This leads to frustration, a lack of time to be collaborative and ultimately it leads to burnout. Many people are operating at the edge of burnout with a few weeks' holiday a year providing the temporary relief required to enable them to keep going. In reality, this is unproductive and unhealthy.

Every day I meet brilliant people doing fantastic work, but they are often overworked, exhausted and stressed. Competing priorities cause teams to pull in different directions, frustrations run high, and fast-paced change prevents them being full of vitality and vigour. This leads to reduced productivity and inefficiencies in the team, due to increased stress and suppressed emotions.

Teams need to continually pay attention to stress levels, use emotions as a source of information for decision-making and seek to operate with a healthy level of stress with energy and enthusiasm.

Step 2 of the OPUS Method sets out the three pillars that provide a foundation for a team to have vitality and communicate effectively so you can align and work together in a healthy and productive way. The three pillars are:

1. **Wellbeing** – balancing resilience, stress and workloads.
2. **Energy and emotions** – using them to understand others and influence positively.
3. **Conversation** – verbalising the hidden dynamics of team behaviour.

Chapters 7 to 9 cover these three pillars and highlight how to reveal the hidden dynamics and be more conscious about what is happening in the team and how to influence it positively.

When teams have the confidence to verbalise the non-verbal (and feel psychologically safe to do so), conversation becomes more open, transparent and honest, and everyone knows what they are working with. Conversation is the route to resolving differences of opinion, deepening understanding of each other, and preventing confusion and misunderstandings which are the source of most conflict.

These three pillars provide the foundation for more vitality in teams. By making the unconscious more conscious and verbalising it within the team, you can continuously re-design how the team work together, ensuring that the needs of everyone are met.

Step 3: The Understanding Approach

Historically, we have relied on cognitive information as a source of power. Team leaders and managers were appointed because they were typically the most experienced people and had the most knowledge about how things were done. As organisations become less hierarchical and more project-focused, the relationships within an organisation (and therefore a team) become more complex as they are more distributed and fluid.

In uncertainty, there is no definitive or binary answer. Therefore, leaders need to develop a different skillset that does not only rely on experience and knowledge. In uncertainty, there is often a lack of information, and leaders and teams need to make decisions based on the available information and their experience. When teams collaborate effectively, they combine their knowledge and experience to make better decisions, allowing them to explore and problem solve together.

In Step 3 of the OPUS Method, in Chapters 10 to 12, we explore three levels of non-verbal awareness that provide a foundation for decision-making in uncertainty and increase understanding where there may be ambiguity. Each level of awareness provides a wealth of information that helps you make better decisions that positively impact everyone and enable you to create clarity at times of uncertainty and find a way through perceived chaos and confusion.

These levels of understanding are:

1. **Self-awareness** – how you respond to people and situations and the impact you have.
2. **Relational awareness** – how others relate to each other and to you.
3. **Field awareness** – the wider team, market conditions, your clients and suppliers and what they think, say and do.

Drawing on hidden, non-verbal and often intangible information, you can be guided in a team to make decisions when facts and cognitive information appear to be missing. By raising your non-verbal awareness within the team, you can work with ambiguity and uncertainty, take into account emotions and market awareness, and act in service of the bigger picture.

The Understanding Approach builds on the previous steps of the Organisation Model and the Pillars of Vitality. In this step, we also delve into how to use your body as a source of information for non-verbal behaviour, and we explore what it means to embody your leadership and literally feel it.

You can use the three levels of understanding to know when to change roles (Step 1: The Organisation Model) or when one of the Pillars of Vitality needs more attention or focus. Using a deeper level of understanding at all three levels and switching between all three, you can increase awareness and understanding of a wealth of information that might normally be overlooked.

Step 4: The Stories Blueprint

In addition to the awareness of self, relationships and the field, we make up stories to bridge the gaps of information and then believe those stories to be true, especially at times of uncertainty. We make decisions about people and things emotionally and justify our position repeatedly. Once you have made a decision, you will look for information that backs up that decision and dismiss information that opposes your decision. Much of this is unconscious and therefore you improve or break relationships unwittingly.

Once someone does something you don't like, there is a tendency to break trust and not regain it. Negative assumptions are often made on both sides; boundaries are held firmly and rigidly, or not at all. In this way, you set an unconscious intention to create distance and division.

By being more conscious of the internal stories you create, you validate them through honest, open conversation. By increasing understanding, the team works through differences of opinion and aligns better together. By making these hidden stories more conscious, you create harmony and cohesion in the team instead of distance and disconnection.

In Step 4 of the OPUS Method, in Chapters 13 to 15, we explore each of the different types of story:

1. **Boundaries** – provide clarity and guidelines for team behaviour but can also push people away.
2. **Assumptions** – influence behaviour and set expectations but can cause breakdowns in communication.
3. **Intentions** – determine your success by playing out unconscious beliefs and focus your attention.

For each of these stories, we will reflect on how they improve relationships in your team and where they create distance and division. As human beings, you are not static. Your behaviour changes according to skills, beliefs and experience. When one person in the team changes, it has an impact on the rest of the team, leading to further change.

As a result, teams continually change and therefore need to adapt and operate in an emergent way. However, we often believe teams are static and make assumptions about what we expect, often being surprised by changing behaviour or not believing it.

This step will challenge you to explore your thought processes and how they influence the team. By shining the spotlight on unconscious thought patterns, you will become more aware of how your behaviour impacts the team and how you can use it more positively to create cohesion and alignment in the team.

Conscious team performance

Working in a team can be easy if the team is willing to be open and honest, but the fear of vulnerability often causes the hidden dynamics in the team to remain hidden and unconscious. Teamwork can be enormously rewarding when you have the ability and humility to learn together, from your mistakes as well as your successes. If you make conversation effortless, your team will be more open and honest with each other. How you communicate together as a team determines your ability to work together cohesively.

You can implement any of the four steps in this book in isolation if you wish. Each one in isolation will enhance the way you communicate and collaborate as a team, revealing hidden dynamics of the team and making intangible information clearer and more tangible. However, I recommend that you apply all four steps and integrate them, each one building on the previous step in order to maximise team communication.

These hidden dynamics of team performance are at play in your team unconsciously. By raising awareness of them and fine-tuning how you use them, individually and collectively, you create a better quality of conversation, based on trust, mutual respect and transparency. This will enhance the wellbeing and performance of the team and have a greater impact on your business and the world of work.

In the following chapters, we will explore each of the 12 hidden dynamics that are at play in more detail.

Step 1
THE ORGANISATION MODEL

In which we explore three crucial roles of
a team in alignment...

Key problems/blind spots

Most teams experience some or all of the following problems and sometimes they may not realise they are happening:

- The team may not be fully aligned and may work in silos.
- There may be unclear or misaligned objectives or constantly changing priorities, so the team is constantly fire-fighting issues.
- The leader of the team may need to get too involved in the detail, so the team don't take responsibility for execution.

Hidden dynamics

The three hidden dynamics of the Organisation Model are:

1. Leading from the front.
2. Leading from the middle.
3. Leading from the back.

Outcomes

By implementing the Organisation Model, you will:

- Know how to align your team using three team roles.
- Have more clarity, more direction and more focus.
- Take more responsibility, execute more efficiently and have more accountability for results.

Chapter 4

LEADING FROM
THE FRONT

*In which we discover how to let go of control when
leading from the front...*

Cutting through the noise

My team are responsible for software applications development delivery and support. We have a lot of legacy applications and until recently we lacked a clear strategic direction. It's chaotic at best, and the team are always under pressure with competing and changing business demands.

We had a lot of resistance both within the team and from across the business because no one understood what we wanted to do or how we could possibly do it. We were all pulling in different directions.

When we worked with Jude and the horses, it became obvious that we didn't know what our goals were or how to visualise them because we work in such chaos. So, we built the chaos as an obstacle course and led the horses through it. We learned to be clear on the current focus and to work together to achieve it. We discovered that we could speed up delivery and reduce the chaos by being clearer and more open with each other. Since working with Jude, we give each other more honest feedback and call out where behaviours are helping or hindering the team efforts.

The aha moments with the horses have influenced how the team works together. The team is more willing to have a go at something new, where people had previously resisted or created obstacles. We've moved from being the 'always late never deliver' team to the team that 'knows their capacity and delivers what they say they will'. Every one of us knows how to cut through the noise – we don't always get it right, but we know how to learn and keep trying.

Jane Huntington, Head of Applications Development and Support, Guide Dogs

What leading from the front is and misconceptions

The Organisation Model consists of three critical roles that make up an effective team – leading from the front to provide the clarity of direction, the middle which is concerned with execution and collaboration, and the back which holds the team accountable.

This chapter explores the role of leading from the front. Leading from the front provides the vision for everyone else in uncertainty and helps a team relax. 'Vision is the ability to talk about the future with such clarity it is as if we are talking about the past' (Sinek, 2014). Take a moment to re-read that sentence and feel the energy behind it. It creates an enthusiasm and inspires future possibilities for the team. This is the energy of leading from the front. Yet one of the most common problems in a team is a lack of clarity on where the team are going or a belief that it's not possible, especially in uncertainty.

In fast-paced working environments, with changing priorities, it often feels as though you are being pulled all over the place. It creates confusion, disagreements and tension over competing objectives. Lack of clarity is common when priorities are changing and often, time is not put aside to agree on what the change of direction is, or even if it is necessary. Rushing after the next shiny thing is a distraction that derails even the best of teams.

There is a common misconception that leading from the front is where the power lies in a team. Leading from the front is only one of the roles in a team that contribute to achieving something together. Chapters 5 and 6 will explain the other roles that are equally important. For now, let's explore in more detail how you lead from the front.

Clarity and direction

Somebody has to have a vision, an idea and someone has to make a decision. Where are you going?

Leading from the front requires clarity, direction and sensitivity. Clarity and direction provide the overall vision, goals and direction, so that everyone knows where they are heading. The sensitivity is critical and is often the missing link.

Many leaders have no problem providing clarity and direction because they know where they want to go, and they like to be in control. This lacks sensitivity and shifts into an energy of controlling rather than leading. This is why leaders often tell me that people are not doing what they want them to do. They think they have been clear about what is expected, but they haven't got the buy-in, trust or respect from the team to execute.

Leading from the front therefore requires a balance between being future focused (inspiring possibilities) and holding empathy and understanding in terms of: What is achievable right now, with this team, with their skills, experience and time? And have I got their trust and respect, so that when the direction is clear, people naturally know what they need to do, together?

Leading from the front can be performed by anyone. It's often seen as the primary role of the MD or CEO. It is also a primary role of any leader of a team e.g., a Project Manager. In reality, it's rarely one person who says: 'Ye-ha, off we go, this way!' That will only get you so far. It's an iterative process within the team but ultimately someone has to make a decision and take a stance on what the objectives are and the direction of travel, and that person can change according to the situation, context, environment, skills, experience or personal preferences.

Setting the direction sounds so simple, yet it's one of the hardest things to do. How many times have you sat in a meeting going round and round, wondering what you are trying to achieve? This is a moment where clarity and direction are needed. Anyone can lead from the front at this point but often either everyone tries to, and nobody listens, or else nobody does. This is typical of teams who have lengthy debates, where there is no consensus on who has the final decision on what you are trying to achieve. The quality of listening is crucial and usually missing.

Leading from the front requires you to define clear objectives on both a micro and a macro level. From the overall vision and strategy of a company to the objectives of a meeting or project, clarity and direction are always needed. You can draw on your experience to set objectives that are stretching yet achievable. This is a fine balance and may require adjustment along the way. Setting aggressive targets that nobody buys into is demotivating and will lead to a disengaged or stressed team. This is the overwhelm part of the zone of uncertainty described in Chapter 2.

Everyone responds differently to goals and objectives. Some people like structure in order to know exactly what is expected of them. Others require more space for creativity. Some are driven by aggressive targets and will make sure they achieve them. Some are happy if they achieve 80% because they know it was too big a stretch. Others are demotivated by aggressive targets and would rather have lower targets that they over-achieve. Everyone's motivation is different so part of leading from the front requires you to understand how to engage different personalities and motivations within the team, all at the same time!

It's less about articulating what you personally want, and more about articulating what is needed in service of the bigger picture. I explore more on leading in service of a bigger picture in Step 3: The Understanding Approach, where Chapters 10 to 12 describe the different levels of awareness that help you understand team dynamics and fine-tune your decisions and communication accordingly.

With fast-paced change in most business, priorities often change. Something happens and the team need to flex and respond. In these moments, chaos and confusion often arise, and more clarity is needed. When priorities change, explain why so that everyone understands what the new priorities are and why. Encourage flexibility in the team but be careful not to become chaotic by adapting so quickly that you never finish anything.

When priorities change, teams often hang on to the original priorities as well. This increases workload and causes continuous tension over competing priorities. There is often no consensus on what needs to be dropped to include the new priority, so everyone tries to do everything. This is unproductive and not possible, leading to inefficient working and deadlines being missed. Stress levels and frustration rise, damaging the team performance.

Let go of control

When priorities change, make sure you are clear what has to be let go of, in order for the new priority to take precedence. Leading from the front is often seen as a position of control. In reality, it is the position with the least amount of control of the execution. It is forward-focused, strategic thinking and a position that requires trust and mutual respect with the rest of the team.

One of the most common problems with leading from the front is that when you focus on where you are going, you can't see what is happening behind you. If you trust your team and are clear on what you expect from them, they should communicate with you, so you don't need to keep checking in on them.

Therein lies the issue, because typically teams only communicate when there is a problem. As a result, the leader at the front often feels as though they are leading in a vacuum, with no idea what is happening behind them. This causes you to continually check in on the team. Every time you do this, you stall the momentum of the team. You get dragged into the detail and the drama of everyday problems.

There is often a desire to be included, to avoid being lonely and to be confident that everything is on track. Many leaders of teams want to feel part of the team and the solution, and it can often feel lonely at the front (or 'at the top' if you have a hierarchical structure). The more you get involved in the detail, the more the team learn to default to you. This prevents the team stepping up and taking responsibility for resolving differences and making the tough decisions. This is a common frustration in a team where the leader at the front often wants the team to step up, and the team often want more responsibility but don't take it when it is given.

It is a vicious circle. Instead, when you lead from the front, let go of control and trust that the team will resolve differences without you. Encourage them to do so and provide clarity on what is expected in terms of both outcomes and communication, so you feel involved without taking all the responsibility. The more you focus on the direction of travel and the more you continually re-articulate the vision and direction, the more the team will learn to take more responsibility.

Figure 2: A client leads a horse from the front
© John Cleary Photography 2016

If you get too involved in the detail, let go of control and create space for your team to make decisions without you. When you repeatedly get involved in every decision, the team learn to include you in everything, resulting in more work and more stress for you. If the direction, roles and responsibilities are clear, the team can take more responsibility and will feel more engaged.

When you let go of control, you create space for the team to step up and flourish. If the team are used to being guided top down, they may need support as they take more responsibility.

Create the vacuum

When you set the direction and let go, there is initially a vacuum. There is a tendency to want to fill it and not give space to the team to work out what to do and how to do it. When you have an idea in your head, time is needed from the moment you think it, to the moment you speak it, to the moment the team processes and understands it, to the moment they start to execute.

Sometimes this is a quick process. Sometimes it takes longer. Avoid filling the gap, otherwise you will continue to be dragged into the detail. Give the team time to work out how they respond and what they need to do.

There is a fine line between allowing space versus commanding and running off into the distance. This is where the sensitivity of leading from the front comes in, something that is often overlooked. It requires sensitivity to know how much clarity and direction are needed and how much to check to ensure there is a common understanding and execution.

Create an environment where the communication between the front and the middle is so effortless that it becomes obvious when you are needed and when you are not. Train your team to resolve issues on their own, without you needing to get involved.

It is your responsibility to let go as much as it is for them to step up. If you want your team to step up, let go and create the vacuum for them to do so.

Benefits of letting go

When you let go of control, you empower the team to take more responsibility. You demonstrate trust in the team, and it encourages them to do the same with each other and the wider organisation.

Teams waste time and effort when they engage in lengthy debates and are not aligned on their objectives. Be clear what you want and allow the team to execute. Encourage them to communicate with you in a way that makes you feel confident that everything is on track. Over time, as you build more trust, the team will know when to involve you and when to update you, so you never feel isolated and out of the loop of communication.

Teams develop when they feel empowered because it feels safe for them to stretch out of the comfort zone and lead from the middle. Leading from the front enables you to be more strategic, to seek new opportunities and move the business forward. It is easier for everyone when the roles are clear, and you all play your part. It starts with you at the front.

Providing the vision requires you to let go of the execution and stay focused on moving forward. There is a difference between being lonely and being alone. 'Lonely' has a desire for support whereas 'alone' has a presence that draws people with you. Stand alone at the front, hold the vision and let go of the execution. Trust that the team will follow you and you will never be alone.

Let go to let come

Leading from the front focuses on moving forward. Sometimes we wait for everyone to be aligned before we take the first step. Instead, focus on where you are going, take a step and encourage everyone to come with you. Strong relationships based on trust and mutual respect will encourage the team to step up.

Create space for the team to do their work and resolve their differences. Listen to feedback from the team, re-prioritise when necessary and ensure it is clearly communicated. When you re-prioritise, be clear what you are letting go of in order to bring something else up the priority chain. Don't keep adding new priorities on top of the existing ones. Something has to give. If

47

you don't provide clarity on this, the team will make their own minds up and everyone will have a different point of view. This is where clarity goes awry.

A lack of clarity wastes energy in the team and creates frustration due to competing objectives. The role of leading from the front ensures that everyone knows what is expected of them. Be clear when you don't have all the answers and pull together as a team to seek them. Be open, honest and transparent in communication.

Allow the team to execute from the middle, so you can be forward focused and strategic. In the next chapter, we explore the role of leading from the middle – the execution of team performance.

 If you'd like to explore this chapter with your own team, download the *OPUS Method of Team Performance* workbook from www.judejennison.com/opus and record your reflections and actions.

Chapter 5

LEADING FROM THE MIDDLE

*In which we explore the need to take more
responsibility for execution...*

Synchronising communication

The team stood with Kalle in the field. She refused to move. Individually, everyone was doing everything they could to get her to move. They really wanted her to go through the gate with them. Kalle was waiting for them to be in sync. She was surrounded by six different opinions, and it was confusing. As one person moved forward to show Kalle what she wanted, someone else was moving backwards or standing still. Kalle didn't know where to look so she closed her eyes and tuned them out.

Everyone was focused on Kalle. She had become the problem 'person' in the team. The team had the desire to get Kalle to go through the gate with them, and they were committed to making it happen, throwing everything (individually) they had into the situation. They were willing to try different things and be flexible, but still the team focused on the horse. They all had different ideas on how to get Kalle to move, and none of them were in sync. Nobody was providing clarity of direction, and everyone had lost focus on the gate.

In addition, the energy had become one of control, where the desire to achieve had become greater than the desire to invite Kalle to join them. This was also happening in their workplace. Everyone was doing their best, attached to a specific outcome, but out of sync and stuck in the cycle of problem fixing.

What Kalle wanted was clarity of direction, focus, synchronised communication and to be inspired to join rather than be dominated. I invited the team to take a breath and relax their bodies. The continuous trying had caused tension to rise. The desire to achieve became greater than the desire to be in relationship. The team went quiet; they took a couple of breaths together. Then I asked them all to look towards the gate and on the count of three all walk towards it. One person stood

> *in front of Kalle, the others stood at the sides and one person stood at the back to create some energy. The leader at the front counted aloud: 'One, two, three – go.'*
>
> *Everyone's focus moved from Kalle to the direction they were heading. Suddenly, the intention was clear and aligned. The moment the team looked at the gate, Kalle followed their gaze too. Everyone was calm. Everyone lifted a foot at the same time and took a step. Kalle lifted her foot and in time with their second step, she took her first. The team walked in perfect harmony towards the gate, and Kalle went willingly.*

I'm not a leader

Leading from the middle is one of the things we do least well. There is a tendency to default to a hierarchical model. At its best, this creates a silo mentality where everyone does their own thing, and nobody in the middle takes responsibility for the whole. At its worst, it puts all the responsibility on the leader at the front, who feels they need to get involved in everything and wishes the team would take more responsibility.

Many people only regard themselves as a leader when they lead from the front. People who lead from the middle often tell me they don't consider themselves to be a leader. They quietly get on with what they need to do to achieve their objectives. This is one of the most common mistakes in teams. No wonder teams are siloed if everyone sticks their head down and only communicates when they have to. This approach causes team members to default to the team leader for key decisions or to resolve issues, causing the leader at the front to continually get involved. It becomes a vicious circle.

Leading from the middle is one of the hardest roles in a team because it involves taking responsibility for team success and influencing others, as well as achieving your own objectives. It requires continuous awareness of the whole and how you fit into it, as well as being the conduit of communication and the coach for those around you who need your support. The role is multi-faced and requires enormous skill, focus and humility.

Nobody wants to be seen as a problem to be fixed. Feel the energy of this for a moment. How does it feel to be the 'problem person' in the team? To know that everyone thinks you should be doing something other than what you are doing. Leading from the middle is a coaching and democratic style of leading. It involves effective communication to ensure that everyone stays on track together, and nobody gets left behind or goes off track.

If something needs to be different, it's the role of the leaders in the middle to speak to it and work out how to resolve it. There will always be differences of opinion in a team. Polarised views are healthy because it enables the team to consider things from different points of view and ensure that everyone is included. Polarised views become a problem when people don't feel safe to express their opinions, or when lengthy and heated debates go round and round without resolution.

Teams become chaotic when they over-communicate. They talk over the top of each other, don't listen and everyone has a different opinion. This wastes time, causes confusion, increases frustration and breaks connection. Alternatively, not communicating and becoming withdrawn breaks the relationships in the team and causes disconnection and frustration.

Leading from the middle requires everyone to communicate effectively. Often the middle of the team commits to their own objectives but not to the team objectives and not to each other. Effective leading from the middle requires you to commit to doing what you need to do to achieve the overall team objectives, not only your individual ones, and work collaboratively to help the whole achieve the collective responsibilities.

Step up and take responsibility

If the leader at the front provides the clarity and strategic direction and lets go of trying to be in control of everything, leading from the middle is concerned with execution. It requires you to be focused on the direction, with awareness of the relationships to ensure everyone in the team is inspired, engaged and supported to come with you.

In the case of the team in the example above, they started off with the horse being a 'problem to be fixed and moved'. Once they turned their attention to where they were going (the gate) and were aligned energetically, Kalle was more than willing to engage and go with them. She wanted clarity and alignment before she was willing to engage.

When the leader from the front steps out of the way, the team in the middle need to recognise they are empowered to make decisions and resolve issues without the leader at the front being involved in the detail. This is a two-fold process – where the leader at the front steps out of the detail and creates the vacuum that the team members in the middle need to fill. Don't wait to be asked to take responsibility from the middle. It's an assumed and critical part of the role.

There is often a resistance to step up and take responsibility for fear of being wrong or criticised, particularly at times of change when there is uncertainty. The role of the middle is to take responsibility for decisions, to work with other members of the team to clarify and resolve issues together, and to never lose sight of the leader at the front and therefore the direction of travel.

When teams believe themselves to be empowered, they often take on a mind of their own and forget about the leader at the front. They fail to communicate to them, causing the leader at the front to want to get involved in the detail because they lack feedback. Often the middle will believe something is not possible and will give up. Leaders in the middle should have a wide awareness of what is going on around them. They focus on the front, on what they individually and collectively need to do and also on the bigger picture. We explore this more in Chapters 10 to 12 in the Understanding Approach. Awareness combined with communication is key.

Seek clarity where things are confused. Group consensus is almost impossible so maximum flexibility will be needed in the middle because ultimately there needs to be a decision that everyone commits to.

If you notice something is missing, speak to it. Agree as a team who needs to fill it. Just because you noticed it first doesn't mean it's your responsibility to fill the gap, but it is your responsibility to name it and ensure it is filled if you spot the gap or problem. Don't leave gaping holes or issues unresolved in the team.

Communicate

Communicate. An easy word, but so difficult to execute. Communication is always rife with issues because the hidden dynamics of non-verbal communication are at play in the team, but everyone usually behaves as though those dynamics don't exist!

When the leader at the front steps out of the detail, they don't have sight of everything that is happening in the middle. Often the middle only communicate to the front when things go wrong. This leaves the leader at the front isolated, wondering whether everything is working or is likely to come crashing down at any moment. Don't wait to be asked for an update. Communicate what is working as well as what is not. This will give the leader at the front confidence in you, but also guide them on how far they can stretch the team and when to increase the pace and when to slow down.

In the middle, speak to what is happening for you. Be open and honest about what you are seeing and what your needs are. One of the biggest mistakes in teams is the lack of feedback, or feedback in the form of blame, judgement and criticism. There is a tendency to believe that the team's failure is down to one person who is not doing what you need them to do. They can easily become 'the problem person' (like Kalle in the example above), and this leads to poor relationships, conflict and polarisation. Steps 2 to 4 of this book explain some of the non-verbal information that is available to you to resolve differences of opinion.

Figure 3: A team of people lead a horse through an obstacle course. Note the communication in the middle
© John Cleary Photography 2019

Don't get caught in a spiral of frustration when things are not working. Communicate to the leader at the front so they know when things are on track and when they are not. Communicate, communicate, communicate.

Align

When you take responsibility in the middle and communicate effectively, you have a greater chance of aligning as a team. The role in the middle is to execute what you need to do, together.

Ensure the whole team is moving forward together in the same direction. Make space for differences of opinion and different ways of doing things, but never lose sight of the collective direction. Focus on the agreed direction.

Recognise that there will be different paces and work to keep everyone together. This is challenging when some people work fast, and others are more methodical. Make sure that there is space for everyone in meetings to reflect and process information in the way that they need to. Some people think as they speak; others need to go away, process and come back with their thoughts. Create an environment where everyone thrives.

There will always be differences of opinion in the team. Let go of needing to be right or have your way be the team's way. Instead, explore ways of doing things together and build on each other. Whenever there is tension in a team due to competing objectives and differences of opinion, there is often a heightened state of fear and stress. The tendency is to focus on the differences. Instead, start by focusing on where you are going and where you are aligned. Begin with the team focus: ensure there is agreement on that and build on it, so you stay forward-focused on the direction rather than the problem. As soon as you find yourself going round and round with the same problem, it's an indicator for change.

Build on each other's points of view. Listen to what the other person has to say. Look for what you agree with, and show your agreement. Then add what you want, in addition. For example, there is often tension between sales and delivery. The sales team want to meet their targets, and the delivery team want to deliver a high quality on budget. If you switch the conversation from either/or to both, it creates a different conversation. How can we meet the sales targets and deliver a quality product/service? Without sales, there is nothing to deliver. High-quality delivery makes it easier to keep customers and sell more to them. The two are inextricably linked. Take time to work through your differences, come to a consensus and communicate it to the rest of the team so everyone is always aligned and clear.

If someone is going off course and lagging behind, re-articulate the direction of travel and provide support.

Clarity in chaos

Finding alignment in the team requires constant communication. Clarity is a crucial part of this. It is not something you do once. You can't agree on what is clear and assume everyone knows and agrees. Clarity is a continuous process of ongoing communication, redefining and revising as things change.

People think they have been clear when they have told someone something once. Clarity is something you create repeatedly as a team. Since everyone will have a different perspective, providing clarity from each perspective enables the team to understand priorities and see where the team is getting derailed.

Leading in the middle requires you to communicate so that the whole team have a common understanding, including understanding where there are disagreements. This enables you to know where to focus attention to re-align, where disagreements need to be resolved and where they can be put aside temporarily.

Competing priorities and objectives are confusing and feel chaotic at times. In uncertainty, there will always be missing information. Be clear about what is known and be clear about what is not known as well. Be clear as a team on the key priorities at any given moment, and reinforce those priorities, especially when they are changing fast.

The tension of misalignment causes friction and the role of leading from the middle is to work through it, so everyone stays focused on the strategy, vision and objectives, and everyone feels supported to achieve together.

Support

Supporting each other improves relationships and deepens the connection. It helps others feel valued and reduces pressure on individuals in the team. People often don't ask for support because they consider it to be a weakness and fear rejection. Asking for support demonstrates humility, and it is a sign of strength to recognise where your boundaries and limits are. Yes, it's vulnerable, but when you seek help to navigate through a challenging period, you create an opportunity for others to feel valued and included.

Accept support with good grace. Be clear about the type of support you want; for example, you may want someone to listen as you offload your frustration, or you may want practical support or advice. Be clear about what you want and ask for the appropriate support when you need it.

Offer support to others if you see people in the team struggling. Sometimes sharing a challenge is enough. Other times, someone may welcome your input and advice. Be clear what you are offering and seek to understand what is needed – a friendly ear or advice. If you offer support and it is rejected, don't take it personally. You've demonstrated your desire to support someone; you've demonstrated your commitment to the team.

People often don't offer support because they don't want to be rejected and because they don't want to disempower the other person. The issue of asking for, offering and receiving support is rife with assumptions and self-judgement! Create a culture in your team where support is part of the process of collaborating together.

Everybody matters

Everybody in the team matters. Whilst the middle is often seen as a lesser leadership role, in fact it's where the power truly lies in a team. It's the place of execution, commitment, support and communication. The middle sets the pace and resolves differences of opinion.

The middle is where teams often fall apart. The complexity of communication takes time, something teams often don't give each other. The balance of sticking your head down to achieve what you need to do versus working with the whole team is often not recognised. The strength of the relationships in the team, the commitment to working together in alignment, the willingness to continually have the difficult conversations – these all determine the team's ultimate ability to achieve.

When you find your flow in the team, you can achieve anything together. Whenever teamwork feels awkward and clunky, reflect on what needs to happen to bring back the state of flow. Avoid silos and divides in the team but make space for different ways of doing things.

Make time to work through differences of opinion and seek common understanding, even if you disagree. You may not always resolve all the differences but create clarity around where you are not aligned and the impact of that.

Above all, stay focused on where you are going. Lift your head up and be forward focused so you don't get lost in the detail of fire-fighting issues.

With the best will in the world, people will always go off track. Having someone to hold you accountable can motivate, energise and keep a team focused and that's where we are going next.

 If you'd like to explore this chapter with your own team, download the *OPUS Method of Team Performance* workbook from www.judejennison.com/opus and record your reflections and actions.

Chapter 6

LEADING FROM THE BACK

*In which we discover the subtleties of holding
accountability for team success...*

Having each other's backs

After a management buy-out, we wanted to maximise our respective talents and experience without treading on each other's toes or damaging egos. I'd always been cynical about leadership training because it seemed to be an intellectual process and my experience of leadership was more of a 'felt' sense. Working with the horses you feel your leadership and it enabled me to understand how to embody my leadership.

Back then, I hadn't considered that we need to be working on our teamwork as a board, as well as thinking about the teams that we've got in our business. When Jude explained the three roles of leading from the front, middle and the back, it reso-nated for me initially as a metaphor. In practice, by working with the horses, I learned how the team can support each other in this way, as opposed to seeing leadership as the lonely, heroic leader upon whose shoulders all leadership ultimately rests.

As a result, in Armadillo, we share out the responsibility for leading the business almost unconsciously now, and it has felt very easy for us to switch into different roles when required. I am very aware when I need to step in and lead from the front. I am also aware that when someone else is leading from the front, I can't switch off... they need support from the side and behind. We understand the importance of checking in with each other to see whether, for example, more momentum needs applying from behind.

I hoped we would build even deeper bonds of trust and give each other permission to fail without stigma or judgement, and that has definitely been the case. It's liberating to feel that I can play to my strengths and be valued by the team for what I bring to the table. I feel more in my element, relatively comfortable in the knowledge that leadership in other important domains that aren't my forte are being taken care of by people I respect

> *and trust implicitly. It means I have the freedom to flex further, knowing someone will bring me back to the strategic direction.*
>
> *Knowing we have each other's backs allows us to be more creative and innovative and try new things. What board isn't going to need to do that in the coming years?*
>
> Chris Thurling, Executive Chairman, Armadillo

Who's got your back?

Leading from the back is the third crucial role within the team. It is often overlooked as a position of leadership. True leading from the back is not passive following; it's an active role, designed to make sure that everyone is accountable and on track.

Often the leader at the front will get involved in the detail because they don't have sight of what is happening in the team. Those in the middle can only see where they're going and the closest members of the team to them. Leading from the back provides the eyes and ears of everything. It's the person who sees across the organisation or across the team and knows who and what is on track, who is struggling, and what is slipping. Because they have sight of everything, they know exactly what needs to happen to bring the team back on track. They see when a re-alignment is needed in the middle, or when a reset of priorities and expectations needs to happen at the front.

Typical functions in an organisation that lead from the back are finance, HR and compliance. It can also be a Project Office Manager who is tracking project deliverables and collating the reports. The person who sees everything across the wider organisation or team is in an ideal position to lead from the back. This role is much more than just observation. By noticing things that nobody else sees, communication to the rest of the team is critical to ensure that everyone knows what needs to be done to stay on track.

The leader at the back holds the team accountable for execution, enabling the leader at the front to be freed up to be more strategic and provide the clarity of direction. When the leader at the front fully trusts the person at the back, they let go of needing to get involved in the detailed execution in the middle and can be more strategic.

Who has got your back? Who is rooting for you so much that you know you can be bolder and move forward, knowing that someone has your back and will support and guide you along the way? When the leaders at the front and back work together, they are the bookends of a brilliant team.

Visibility

When the leader at the front focuses on where they are heading and the strategic direction, they don't always know what is happening behind them. The leader at the back has visibility of everything. They have an understanding of the big picture, they see what needs to be done, and they communicate with the leader at the front, so that everyone is always in sync.

Other members of the team may look to the leader at the back for a second opinion, because they can give feedback within the context of the bigger picture and provide a more objective point of view. In this role, you need to be in sync with the leader at the front, to know exactly what is required, what the objectives are and how everyone in the team fits into that. If the leader at the back is out of sync with the front, chaos can ensue in the middle.

At the back, your role is to ensure that everyone knows exactly what they need to do to achieve the team objectives. You see where communication is breaking down, where someone is going off track, where objectives are being missed. You also start to pre-empt issues that might arise in future because you see the trends.

If someone is falling behind or struggling, the leader at the back will notice and be able to see what needs to be done to bring that person back on track. That person may need support from the middle, they may need support from the back, they may need time out for personal reasons, and someone else may need to step in. Sometimes the objectives may need to be re-defined because changing priorities mean that the original plan is no longer achievable. The leader at the back misses nothing and ensures action is taken so the direction remains clear.

Leading from the back is a more operational role and is the perfect partner to the more strategic style of leadership from the front. When both are completely in sync, the whole team are clear what they need to do.

Accountability

Another responsibility of leading from the back is to hold the team accountable. Is everyone doing what they said they would do? If not, what needs to happen? In this role, because you have sight of everything, you can provide feedback to the team or the individuals who need to do something different. You also need to provide feedback to the person leading from the front. They need to know if the pace is too fast or too slow or if objectives or deadlines are going to be missed.

At the back, you see the differences of opinion. The leader at the back can and should facilitate alignment discussions within the team where needed, to ensure competing objectives and disagreements are resolved. This ensures that the focus stays on moving forward rather than getting stuck in the middle, going round and round having the same debates.

Accountability ensures that everyone knows what they need to do and provides support to the whole team to keep everyone on track. There is a delicate balance required from the back that is not too dominant and aggressive in holding accountability and not too passive in allowing people to be let off the hook.

Accountability requires sensitivity to know when to challenge and when to support. The team need to know that there is appropriate challenge and support. The leader at the back needs to have the courage and compassion to know when to challenge and hold the team accountable when they under-achieve and when to support the team when what they are trying to do is not possible.

Figure 4: A team of people demonstrate the three roles – front, middle and back. Note the legs are synchronised with the horse at the front, side and back
© John Cleary Photography 2016

Energy and momentum

Another role of leading from the back is to provide the energy and momentum for the team. We will explore this in more detail in Chapter 8. The leader at the back reminds everyone of deadlines approaching, ensures timekeeping and discipline are adhered to and recognises when the team need time to reflect or space to be creative.

If the team starts to lose momentum, it's your role at the back to re-invigorate the team, to provide enthusiasm for the team objectives and ensure everyone stays engaged. By contrast, you can remind people to slow down when they are getting tired and stressed.

When teams are under pressure, there tends to be an 'always-on' approach that can escalate, increase stress and lead to burnout. The leader at the back can prevent this by noticing the energy of the team, see who is struggling, identify who has spare capacity and decide what needs to happen to keep the team engaged without burning them out.

Often, leading from the back is seen as the person who drives everyone and makes everything happen. They create the energy and push hard – for example, finance may put the pressure on to achieve the financial targets; operations will drive the sales teams to meet their targets or push delivery to meet their deadlines. Too much passion or too much drive and commitment create coercion or constant nagging and the leader at the back can become dominant and bullying. This is not effective leadership from the back!

Instead, the leader at the back needs to have the ability to fine-tune their approach, to have empathy and compassion for the team, to have energy and enthusiasm for what the team are trying to achieve, and to have the sensitivity to know when to increase the energy and when to lessen it, so it is always appropriate for the situation.

Continuing to push a burned-out team to meet unrealistic objectives lacks the finesse of leadership that is so crucial at the back, and an awareness of the wellbeing of the team as outlined in Chapter 7 is an essential part of the role.

Commitment

The leader at the back needs to be committed to both the team and the objectives. Often, they are committed to the objectives and lose sight of what it takes to commit to the team. This means finding the delicate balance between knowing when to challenge and generate energy and momentum, and when to ease off, provide support, empathy and compassion, and know that what needs to happen is a change in the objectives because they are not achievable for whatever reason.

The leader at the back is therefore the voice of commitment to both the team and the objectives. They need to navigate the delicate balance between results and relationships. They are also responsible for ensuring that everyone else in the team stays committed to both.

Teams are often more committed to the objectives than they are to each other. This is a common cause of tension in the team, where differences of opinion don't get resolved because the focus is on what you want to achieve personally, rather than collectively. I cover this in more detail in Chapter 15 on intentions.

I've got your back!

Leading from the back is traditionally seen as the driving force for the team. This is partially true, and hopefully you see that it takes skilful emotional intelligence and sensitivity to know when to drive and challenge and when to provide support with empathy and compassion.

It is much easier to work in a team when you know someone has your back. If the leader at the back builds respect in the team, the team will rely on them to call out things that they may not see when they are stuck in the detail.

Accountability, energy and commitment should not be full on, flat out to the point of burnout. They should be constantly flowing and flexing according to the individuals, the relationships, the situation and the objectives. Holding the picture of both the team and objectives is therefore critical at the back, to ensure alignment and wellbeing of the team.

If you'd like to explore this chapter with your own team, download the *OPUS Method of Team Performance* workbook from www.judejennison.com/opus and record your reflections and actions.

Step 2
THE PILLARS OF
VITALITY

In which we explore the three pillars of non-verbal behaviour that create vitality in the team…

Key problems/blind spots

Most teams experience some or all of the following problems and sometimes they may not realise they are happening:

- They may be stressed or trying to keep going under pressure.
- They may have differences of opinion, leading to frustration and unresolved emotions.
- They may use energy inefficiently by wasting energy on being bored, frustrated or overwhelmed.

Hidden dynamics

The three hidden dynamics of the Pillars of Vitality are:

1. Wellbeing
2. Energy and emotions
3. Conversation

Outcomes

By implementing the Pillars of Vitality, you will:

- Reduce stress and improve wellbeing and productivity.
- Use emotions and energy as a source of information to positively influence the team.
- Elevate the quality of conversation to reveal and understand the hidden dynamics of teamwork, improving the relationships within the team.

Chapter 7

WELLBEING

In which we recognise the need to slow down to speed up...

Admitting to exhaustion

A team walked through my gate. For 18 months, they had undergone a major organisational restructure. The culture of the organisation was to adapt rapidly to change, but the incessant nature of it was taking its toll. As the team arrived, I felt a wave of exhaustion overcome me that had not been there before. It was literally oozing out of them, and I could feel it.

The horses were in the front paddock close to the gate. They looked up. One by one, the horses lay down and closed their eyes.

'Wow, are they tired?' someone asked.

'I don't know,' I replied. 'Are you?'

'Yes,' came the reply. 'I wish I could lie down and rest!'

One by one, the team admitted how exhausted they were. They were reluctant to admit to it because their company culture was to be resilient, and they equated being resilient with pushing through and not admitting to being tired. There was shame in being seen to not cope.

Once they had named their exhaustion, the horses all stood up again. They had made their point. As crazy as this may sound, the horses have repeatedly demonstrated the energy of a team on arrival, galloping around, bucking and rearing when clients bring stress and tension, and standing quietly dozing by the gate when clients are calm.

Exhaustion is information

Exhaustion has become normalised in the workplace. Most people are frantically juggling work and home priorities, with a lack of time to pay attention to self-care. Increased workloads and an 'always-on' mentality lead to failing to switch off and get an appropriate amount of rest. High volumes of change lead to increased pressure at work and in many cases failing to switch off fully leads to a long-term lack of sleep.

In parallel, many organisations create a tacit expectation that if you cannot cope with the workload or the volume of change, you are not resilient enough, not flexible enough and not adaptable enough. The expectation to be resilient shifts the burden of blame from employer to employee and is causing a mental health crisis at work.

The increased focus on resilience in the workforce can be damaging as people stop being honest about what is an acceptable level of work. When Covid-19 hit in 2020, everyone was stressed, and everyone responded in different ways. Many leaders were surprised at who in their team coped and who didn't. The pandemic hit at a time when the world was already overwhelming. Political polarisation, climate change, poverty, high workloads, as well as busy personal lives – children, ageing parents, ill health. The list of stresses on us in our society is enormous. No wonder the whole world was in overwhelm.

Pace

The pandemic required a rapid response for businesses to survive. In a crisis, we sometimes have to act fast, and that requires everyone to go at full speed. It's not sustainable long term though, and sometimes it's better to be more measured and think things through. Notice the default pace of your team. Do you consciously change it, or is super-fast your unconscious default and therefore the only pace?

Everyone will have a different preferred pace, and this is challenging in a team of people who all have different preferences. Is the pace of your team too fast or too slow for you? What about for others in the team? Are they struggling to keep up or itching to go faster? Somehow you need to find the ideal team pace and vary it according to changing needs.

If you are someone who works at a fast pace, you may assume that everyone can keep up with you. That might not be the case so pay attention to who is keeping up and who you are losing along the way. Teams burn out if the pressure is always on. If you are someone who goes flat out until you keel over, consider how you can have a more measured pace, so it doesn't feel like an endurance race for others who work with you, and so you don't burn out.

Too much speed prevents creativity and innovation. It also doesn't allow for time to process learning. Notice where your pace is a default pattern of behaviour and consider what is the most appropriate pace long term as well as short term. Often, we have learned to work at a particular pace and don't always know that it doesn't serve us or the team.

If you are someone who likes to take time to reflect and consider things from different angles, you may want to move at a slower pace. At times, you may need to speed up to keep up with the team and at other times, you may want to slow the team down, invite them to reflect and make sure that everything is being considered.

Explore how you create space for you to process and reflect, if this is your preferred style, without holding the whole team up. For those who work best at a faster pace, they need space to be able to do so. Don't hold them back but remind them to slow down to recharge and to ensure that everyone has a voice (including you).

Fast is not always best although there is a tendency to hold this as a belief in today's fast-paced business environments. Pace is always tricky because it varies for everyone, and misunderstandings often occur when the pace is mismatched. There are times when we need a faster pace and times when we need a slower pace. The pace needs to flex continually within the team. Particularly in the current work environments, where a fast pace is a given for most people, there is a need to pay attention to the pace. Make sure that everyone is working in sync and the pace suits the whole team, not just a few.

There is no right or wrong with the pace. The mood of the team, the energy, the objectives, deadlines and personal styles will all influence the pace that is needed. The more awareness you have of the collective team pace and the individual paces within the team, the more you can flex it, and the more effective the whole team will be, together.

A continual fast pace may be the default but ultimately will lead to everything being a priority and create high volumes of stress which are not sustainable or productive in the long term. Whatever pace you go at, choose it consciously and wisely, and choose a pace that allows you to flex to meet the needs of everyone.

Above all, find a pace that enables the whole team to be aligned and in sync.

Stress behaviour

At times of disruptive change and uncertainty, the need to move fast can lead to stress behaviour and even depression, anxiety, fear, frustration or sadness. Stress can cause people to become withdrawn, irritable and inflexible, and this has a negative impact on team cohesion. If you and your team are operating with high levels of stress, you'll be less efficient and productive. That means it will take you longer to do everything. Consider that for a moment. If you go too fast to a point of stress, it will take longer. Even strong relationships may become tense and disagreements may go unresolved.

Stress causes an impact on your body and mind. Many people are so used to pushing through that it becomes the norm. They carry on, permanently depleted, not realising that they are less productive, and not realising they are stressed.

Alternatively, people may become withdrawn and cease to put their opinions forward because they can no longer be bothered. It's too much effort to have the fight, so they withdraw instead. This can lead to people feeling less engaged and less committed because it has all become too much effort and they are depleted.

Eventually, these people will leave the organisation because it is easier to walk away than to try to maintain the pace and deal with the associated stress in the team. It's easy to overlook these people because they are often the quiet ones.

Others might try to proactively reduce stress through exercise, healthy eating, meditation and more sleep. This can be helpful but only if the workload is manageable. Otherwise, this puts additional stress on people as they believe they 'should' be able to cope and on top of a high workload, you've added a long list of wellbeing 'things to do'!

If the workload or pace continue to be unrealistic, the team will continually under-perform. It is a team responsibility to manage the wellbeing and stress of the whole team. Check in with each other regularly and find ways to ease the pressure. Re-prioritise, re-focus and re-commit to the new priorities. Be clear what needs to change to reduce stress in the organisation. Be aware that continuing to push through will cause burnout and prevent you from achieving optimum performance.

In January 2017, the UK government commissioned the Stevenson–Farmer independent review into mental health in the workplace (Stevenson, 2017). The review aimed to understand how employers can better support employees, including those with poor mental health or wellbeing. In October of the same year, Deloitte (Siegel, 2017) was asked to support the review by exploring the cost of poor mental health to employers and the return on investment for mental health interventions. The Deloitte report calculated the cost of poor mental health in the workplace to be £33bn–£42bn, approximately 2% of UK GDP. The average return on investment of workplace mental health interventions was a ratio of 4:1.

I cannot emphasise enough the need to take stress and workloads seriously to maintain long-term wellbeing and team performance. Something has to give – either the health and wellbeing of the team, or the priorities and results. Most teams choose to make results more important than wellbeing. It's time to bring that back into balance.

Resilience has limits

Companies spend millions on wellbeing. It is a growing industry, but most wellbeing initiatives are a sticking plaster on an unrealistic level of workload and pressure. Working practices and the leadership of the organisation are major contributing factors to work-related stress. The *Mental Health at Work 2019* report (BITC, 2019, p. 8) cites that '62% of managers faced situations where they put the interests of their organisation above the wellbeing of colleagues'.

No wonder employees are weary. Resilience has limits, and how you lead has a major impact. If you implement wellbeing programmes at huge cost to the organisation without reviewing leadership and teamwork in the organisation, you may not see a change in levels of stress.

Resilience training, however well-meaning, often creates the expectation that employees should dig deeper whilst simultaneously being put under more pressure. This is not sustainable or reasonable. There is a time and a place for pushing through in a crisis or for a specific deadline but it's not an ideal long-term strategy.

High-performing leaders and teams are often exhausted, overworked and stressed. They often cease to realise it because they've learned to suppress exhaustion and stress in a bid to be resilient. In the process of shutting down, they lose their vitality and vigour. People struggle on because they think they should and eventually keel over. Work-related stress rarely happens suddenly. It builds up over months, but it often takes people by surprise because they've learned to suppress emotions for the sake of the team results.

Silicon Valley futurist and business consultant Alex Soojung-Kim Pang dispels the myth that the harder we work, the better the outcome: 'Deliberate rest restores your energy, gives you more time, helps you do more, and helps you focus on the things that matter most while avoiding those that don't' (Pang,

2018, p. 246). Making time to recharge and reduce the pressure of work is crucial for the long-term performance of the team.

In fact, a team who work fewer hours but are more focused will be more productive. Years ago, I had a health problem that required me to reduce my hours to only five hours a day. At the time, I was regularly putting in 12-hour days and leading a European team. I was anxious about not letting the team down by my reduced hours.

At the end of three months, my boss confirmed that he had not noticed any difference in the quality and quantity of my output and my team hadn't either! Instead, I'd prioritised so well because I had to. If it was not business critical, I let it go. Every minute that I was working was highly productive. Meetings I joined were focused and short. It was a great lesson in discovering how to be more productive in less time.

Before a team can be high-performing, you need to tackle stress levels. People don't get stressed because they are not capable. The reasons are many and varied but the most common ones are unattainable targets, unachievable workload, changing priorities and unresolved disagreements. Understand the root cause, have compassion for yourself and the team, and seek to resolve the real issue. Remember that everyone is doing their best, and stress will impact behaviour, productivity and therefore results.

Wellbeing is a leadership and team issue

The Global Risks Report 2019 (Collins, 2019) published by the World Economic Forum highlighted 'Heads and Hearts' (p. 32) as one of the top five risks in 2019. Specifically, it cited a decline in empathy and a rise in anger and explained that 'a common theme is that psychological stress is related to a feeling of lack of control in the face of uncertainty' (p. 34).

This is stress behaviour and is unsustainable. With increasing uncertainty due to fast-paced change in business, the emotional wellbeing of the team is crucial and it is a responsibility of the collective to support each other at times of stress. This may require re-prioritising and letting go of attachment to everything being critical.

Continuous change requires greater flexibility in an organisation. There is a need to review the strategic direction and shift quickly in response to both organisational change and market conditions. Teams perform at an optimal level when they have a sense of purpose, work that is meaningful, and a level of stress that gives them the edge, rather than tipping them over it. Vitality of the team is the first critical stage of recovery and most often overlooked. Teams and organisations must explore new ways to create a vibrant workforce, minimise stress and generate vitality so that everyone thrives.

Talk to your team about how they cope with change. Make space for people to rejuvenate and maintain their energy. The business case for wellbeing at work is clear. Continually putting people under pressure with unachievable workload and targets causes stress behaviour, which impacts productivity and denigrates relationships. Have open conversations about stress and behaviour without blame, judgement or criticism and take action to address the overall wellbeing of the team.

Wellbeing is a team issue, a leadership issue and an organisational issue. Business can solve all of the world's problems if employees are full of vitality and vigour. You can and should consider it a top priority in your team.

 If you'd like to explore this chapter with your own team, download the *OPUS Method of Team Performance* workbook from www.judejennison.com/opus and record your reflections and actions.

Chapter 8

ENERGY AND EMOTIONS

In which we explore how energy and emotions provide the foundation for actions...

The impact of energy and emotions

I was so excited to be Jude's first test client that I had envisaged making a deep and immediate connection with her horse Kalle. I'd only ever admired horses from afar, but I was so full of hope that I'd almost imagined riding off into the sunset with an everlasting bond.

I stepped into the arena with this massive and beautiful beast... and it was terrifying. I wanted so badly to build a bond but every time Kalle flinched, I jumped out of my skin, which made her do the same. Kalle's hooves seemed so huge and I was sure she was going to trample me. The harder I tried to connect, the more I flinched, and my energy grew to such a state of intensity that I couldn't stop crying. As I got my breath at the side of the arena, I felt defeated and disillusioned.

'Do you want to try again?' Jude asked me. Whether I imagined it or not, I felt a disappointment. Jude believed in her work so much that she had risked her whole career to provide this experience for clients. I wanted to support her, not prove her wrong.

'No,' I said, 'Give me a minute.' I felt exhausted. But with that came a release of pent-up energy and I felt a sudden calmness. Jude told me to place one hand on Kalle's chest and another on her back. 'You won't be able to match her breathing as hers is much slower but lean in and try to slow your breathing to her pace.'

I nervously sidled up to Kalle and reached my arms around her. I felt her heartbeat, I felt her breath and I tried to slow to her rhythm. With that, Kalle dropped her head deep into my chest. It was a cathartic moment as we connected.

I learned how to manage my energy in order to connect and by the end of the day, Kalle was following me loose around the arena. I learned some invaluable lessons about myself which I

> *have carried forward into my speaking and presenting work. I don't need my energy to be full on; in fact, when I release some of that intense energy, I am even more effective. It was a pivotal moment for me.*
>
> Michelle Mills-Porter, MD

Making sense of emotion

Michelle's existential anxiety in uncertainty flipped her almost instantly into a state of overwhelm. By creating space to process her emotional response, she was able to bring herself back out of the overwhelm and into her leadership. By being honest about her emotion, Michelle was able to use it as a source of information. Instead of suppressing her emotion and it being a hidden dynamic, her transparency enabled us to work together to help her release the pent-up stress and move through it.

Once the stress no longer had a hold over her, Michelle was able to influence the horse from a calm state of confident leadership, and in so doing, she learned how to use her energy and emotions to influence others in her life and work.

I often invite clients to start a meeting by using one word to describe their emotion. For some people, this is really difficult because they often don't have the language to describe how they feel because they've never considered it before. I encourage people to listen to their body, so they sense into how they physically feel because the physical response in your body provides information on your emotions. For example, some people will feel anxiety as a knot in their stomach; others will feel anxiety first in their chest. By understanding your emotional state at any one time, you can start to use your emotions as a source of information.

Understanding team emotions

Ria Blagburn from Vanti explains how they have created a culture where people in the team share openly and honestly about their emotions and how it helps them work together better:

We recognise that how people feel and what is happening in their lives has an impact on their work as well. That's why we start every meeting with a brief check-in. We ask everyone to say how they feel and that informs us as a team. For example, if a new parent says they have been awake all night with a new-born baby, we know they will be more tired and might not be as creative as on a day when they've had a good night's sleep. It helps them be able to say that they feel tired because they have been awake all night.

By doing this, the team has an understanding of how everyone else feels and can work with them without getting frustrated. It makes the team more human and has enabled people to be more honest about their emotions. If someone in the team is struggling with mental health issues, they know they can talk to someone in the team. The team will check in on each other and it leads to greater understanding and greater harmony in the team.

Obviously, we balance this with results because we have to get the work done as well, but at least we show compassion for people. When people first join the team, they find it strange, but over time, by normalising emotion as a fundamental part of human behaviour, they know that they can be themselves. As a result, people are more authentic and engaged in the business.

In a team, there is often a wide range of emotions in response to the same activity or meeting. Some people get excited about analysing data in a spreadsheet whereas for others, this can send them into a state of overwhelm and panic. Some people feel excited about a presentation; others are terrified and others are bored because they've done it so many times before. It often surprises people that their emotional responses vary considerably in response to the same activity or experience. They may have never considered that everyone in the team responds differently.

Your emotions may be impacted by external events and people, but they are also impacted by your personal preferences, experiences and how you respond out of your comfort zone. For those who don't like being out of their comfort zone or in an unpredictable environment they may be tipped into overwhelm, as Michelle was. There is a tendency to make overwhelm wrong, especially when only one person in the team is feeling it, but it is a source of information to keep you safe.

By paying attention to the different responses within the team, you can make decisions that work for the whole team rather than just for you. How I work with Michelle would be different from how I work with someone who is excited to dive in and not in overwhelm. Being honest about how you feel in a team is crucial for decision-making.

Energy as information

Your emotional state influences your energy. In addition, your values, beliefs, experience and many other factors also influence your energy. The moment clients walk through my gate, the horses pay attention to their energy and respond accordingly. Clients are completely oblivious to this of course, but I get a sense immediately of how the team feel, emotionally and energetically, by seeing how the horses respond.

If the horses move to the far end of the field, it might mean that the team are highly anxious. If the horses come over, it often indicates that the team are calm, build strong relationships and have compassion.

**Figure 5: Mr Blue (left) and Gio playing with excitement,
in response to the energy of a team**
© John Cleary Photography 2018

This provides powerful information that clients may believe is hidden and may be different from the words they say. If you've ever walked into a dodgy part of town and felt unsafe, you're sensing into the energy of the location. This awareness keeps you safe. Similarly, if you walk into a meeting room, you get a sense immediately of who is bored, who is engaged, who is switched off, who is anxious. This is more difficult in a virtual working environment, but if you slow down and sense into the energy of a team meeting, you can recognise the different energies.

Of course, be careful if you are making assumptions about the energy. You may need to test it out with the team. We will explore this further in Chapter 14 on assumptions.

Energy is often a dynamic of a team that the team believes is hidden. In reality, the energy of the team is continuously influencing behaviour, often unconsciously. When the whole team is fully aware of the individual and collective energy within the team, you can use it to find a state of flow. You all sense when you are in flow; you build on each other's actions, sensing non-verbally and energetically what is needed in any given moment.

It's easy to forget that there is a wealth of information available to you. In moments of doubt, confusion or uncertainty, pay attention to the energy of the team, and see how you can alter the energetic state to something that is relevant for any given moment.

Different levels of energy

Often people think about energy in terms of high energy – enthusiasm, commitment, a fast pace, excitement, joy. This is one type of energy of course, but energy comes in many different forms. Being aware of your own energy and the energy of the team and knowing how to flex it is a crucial skill that is rarely taught, but it's one of the most skilful things you can use in your leadership toolkit.

The high energy of enthusiasm motivates and energises you and influences others, usually in a positive way. It can also exhaust people if you are full on all the time. The energy of your team has a huge impact on your ability to achieve as a team. If someone is out of sync, this will create a break in the flow of the team. That's why it's important to have an awareness both of your own energy and of the energy of others so you can decide what needs to happen to bring the team back in sync.

It's not authentic to always have high energy. There will be times when someone in the team is grieving and needs space for this, or when someone is exhausted because they were awake all night, or because their workload has been incessant for weeks. Pushing through is not authentic behaviour, and your energy will be at odds with the pushing-through action. When energy is lower, other members of the team need to give each other space and potentially pick up some of the workload. The energy of individuals and the collective informs how the team lead each other from the middle and is a continual state of fine-tuning and re-adjustment.

If the energy is flat, consider what is behind that. Is it exhaustion because you've been flat out for weeks without a break to recharge? Is it flat because the work is not interesting, or the team are not engaged? Or perhaps everyone is tired of having the same debate and never resolving the real (often hidden or unstated) issue?

Sense into what is happening and make decisions that benefit the whole team. If everyone is exhausted, taking the pressure off everyone for a moment will enable them to recharge. If it's flat because there is apathy, you may want to inject some enthusiasm and find ways to re-engage everyone.

Does the work need to be more meaningful or more purposeful? Or do people need a break? Consider where the zone of uncertainty described in Chapter 2 has an effect on the energy of the team as well.

Reveal the hidden energy

Your energy is oozing out of you all the time and impacting your team. It's not really hidden at all! Pay attention to your own energy and to the energy of the team and make decisions according to what is needed to find optimal team performance. Notice where your own energy is out of sync with the team and make a decision about what needs to happen.

Energy and emotions influence behaviour, often unconsciously. Be aware of how energy and emotions influence you and others. Use them as a source of information to guide your decisions and actions. Notice how your boredom influences others. You may need to self-manage if you are the only person in the meeting who is bored, or you will quickly drag the team down with you.

However, if everyone is bored, then it's time to shake things up. We've all sat in boring meetings and there is nothing to be gained by doing so. If everyone in a meeting is bored, you have all contributed to it. Often everyone will sit in a boring meeting and blame everyone else, or even blame the meeting, as if it is a sentient being! If you're bored, do something about it and take responsibility for changing the energy and emotion in the team.

Balance the energy and pace so that it is appropriate for the task in hand and capabilities of the team. High energy and enthusiasm can lead to burnout if it is not balanced with quieter moments of calm reflection. Where there are disagreements, notice where the tension rises and explore ways to bring more calm into heated debates.

Heated debates are not necessarily wrong as they in themselves generate energy to build on, as long as they are done without blame, judgement or criticism. We will explore this further in the next chapter as we look at how we can use conversation to reveal further hidden dynamics within the team.

 If you'd like to explore this chapter with your own team, download the *OPUS Method of Team Performance* workbook from www.judejennison.com/opus and record your reflections and actions.

Chapter 9

CONVERSATION

In which we turn non-verbal behaviour into powerful conversations…

The voice of a power struggle

John (not his real name) led Kalle round the arena. He held the lead rope about a foot away from her face and tugged it forcibly. Kalle headbutted him hard on the shoulder. He pushed her face back with his arm. She headbutted him again. Surprisingly, Kalle walked with him, but it was a constant power struggle as they walked around the arena.

Kalle constantly headbutted John, and John shoved her back. Both of them raised their energy and shoved harder. I was uncomfortable watching and considered stepping in. I didn't want John to get knocked off his feet, and Kalle was getting more forceful in her shoving of him, as he was of her.

I held back because I trust Kalle to not hurt anyone. Usually if someone yanks her about, she refuses to move. This time, I recognised that she was making a point, and I could feel the frustration in the team who were stood watching with me.

When John and Kalle came back to the group, I asked: 'How was that?'

John replied: 'It was fine. I got the job done.' Kalle headbutted him hard again.

I said: 'How do you think that was for Kalle?'

'She did it, didn't she?'

'Do you think she enjoyed it?' I probed.

'She must have done,' came the reply.

I asked the team to say what they saw without judgement or criticism.

'I saw Kalle headbutt you and you shove her back. I saw you both pushing and shoving all the way round.' John looked surprised and said: 'Did she? I didn't notice.' One of the team said: 'This is common for you, John. When we tell you something, you often don't recognise it.'

John went quiet for the rest of the day. He was in deep reflection. He'd had a hard lesson early on in the day, and I took the pressure off him to allow him to reflect.

At lunchtime, John said to the group: 'You are always telling me I don't listen, but I never agreed. Now I understand why. I didn't listen to Kalle, I don't listen to the team, and I feel bad about it. I need to change that.'

John had physically felt the impact of not listening and for the first time understood how all of his relationships at work were challenging because of it. He resolved to make changes.

Three months later, John and the team told me that John listened better, and the team were supporting him, without the previous frustration they had felt and without blame, judgement and criticism. Changing behaviour is a team effort. When a team replace judgement and frustration with challenge and support from a place of respect and connection, they can help each other change their behaviours that are deeply ingrained. This is conversation in action.

Non-verbal feedback is information

All feedback is information. It guides us to make change. John's power struggle with Kalle was a non-verbal conversation. Both of them wanted something different. Once John learned to feel the discomfort of the power struggle with Kalle, he understood it and was more able to recognise future non-verbal feedback more easily.

Some of the most powerful feedback is non-verbal. You give and receive micro feedback non-verbally moment by moment. The flick of your eyes, a sideways glance, someone shifting in their seat, leaning forward with enthusiasm, your energy and emotions are all feedback.

Non-verbal feedback provides additional information that can guide you or others to do things differently. If someone is shifting in their seat, they are communicating something. Perhaps they are bored, or eager to contribute, or disagree and want to express it? There are many reasons, but they indicate something is needed. What might that be? Instead of ignoring their discomfort, ask them what they need or want.

By bringing conscious awareness to what you are sensing, feeling and thinking, you can use the information to decide what you say and do next. By verbalising the non-verbal behaviour, you create more transparency in your communication. Having a conversation can reveal the hidden dynamics of non-verbal behaviour and ensure that everyone in the team has a common understanding. This will minimise frustration and misunderstanding in the team and help you align.

Non-verbal feedback is often misconstrued. Have you ever sat in a meeting and seen someone shift in their seat and not been sure whether they disagree or want to interject? Non-verbal communication is rife with making assumptions, which we will explore further in Chapter 14. Pay attention to how your body feels in response to what you are sensing and seeing. Your own physical response can guide you, based on the energy you pick up.

In the same way as you use non-verbal cues to guide you, other people experience your non-verbal cues. Your energy, your body, your movements indicate information about how you feel and provide others with an opportunity to act and speak based on what they see and experience from you.

You have non-verbal conversations all the time, most of the time unconsciously. Often people think they are hiding what is going on internally but once you start paying attention to non-verbal communication, you will notice it more and more. By raising awareness of what you feel energetically, emotionally and physically in your body, you create a more conscious conversation in the team by articulating what you are sensing and improve the quality of your relationships through greater understanding.

If you are not happy about a decision, speak to it. Don't sit in silence and complain later. Articulate how you feel about things and try to make sense of the cognitive information that the emotion brings. You may still need to go along with a team decision, but at least by articulating how you feel about it, you allow space for everyone to understand your position and explore an alternative perspective.

Use emotion to guide conversation

How do you know when you are frustrated? What do you sense in your body? Perhaps you have tension in your stomach, or maybe it starts in your chest. Instead of avoiding it and ignoring it, be curious about it. You may believe that you hide your frustration, but others sense it in you, just as you sense it in them!

Frustration (in you or others) is feedback that something is not in flow. Perhaps someone is not doing what you want them to do, or maybe you are out of sync with the rest of the team. Feeling frustrated with others is unlikely to resolve the issue and more likely to cause a greater divide in a relationship.

Instead, use the frustration as a pointer to be curious about what needs to happen. Does the other person need something from you that you are not providing? Are your objectives out of sync? If so, have a conversation about that.

Often, we are very clear what we don't want but less clear about what we do want. The following process turns your non-verbal experience into a verbal conversation that improves the relationship and articulates your needs. The first three steps are your internal process; the fourth one is what you might say to the team. For example, if someone is going off topic in a meeting and you find yourself getting irritated, here's how it might go:

1. Internally: How do I feel?
   I'm feeling frustrated.

2. Internally: What is the frustration about?
   Someone is going off at a tangent and I'm irritated that the meeting will go on too long or we won't get everything done.
   Note: The tendency might be to want to blame or judge the other person for always talking too much. Avoid judgement and stick to the facts.

3. Internally: What do I want or need?
   I want to get through the meeting without going off at a tangent. I want to cover the other important things we have to discuss. I've got a lot of work to get on with and I don't like long meetings.

4. Verbally: What is my request?
   I know this is an important point that we need to resolve. I want to make sure that we have time to cover everything on the agenda. Can we park this for now and come back to it later/in another meeting?

Often everyone will heave a sigh of relief because you've articulated what more than one person is thinking. These steps take the emotion out of the conversation but use the emotion as a source of information to guide a transparent conversation. In the process, you acknowledge what you and others want and need, and are then clear what your request is. There is no need for blame, judgement or criticism here. You acknowledge that something is important and make sure that the focus is where it needs to be.

In this way, the person receiving the feedback is empowered to make decisions without the shame of being made wrong. When you give feedback in a clean way without blame, judgement and criticism, it enables you to work together to solve a situation rather than expecting one person to change.

This has a much more powerful impact than getting irritated about the amount of time a discussion is taking. Using this approach, you verbalise the hidden non-verbal communication and create a conversation that is more meaningful, aligned and improves the relationships based on mutual understanding.

If feedback from others towards you is emotional, consider what that person is wanting from you. What is their need that is not being articulated? What was the impact that you had without realising it? What is their request of you really? You can reverse engineer the steps on the previous page to understand what their request is. Or be curious and explore it together, without assumptions.

Don't get caught in the emotion of others and don't take feedback personally. It is one person's perspective. 'While all personal feedback is not true, I believe all personal feedback is relevant' (Taylor, 2017). Accept feedback graciously, whether it is positive or negative. There is always a tiny amount of truth in feedback, even if you don't agree with it. Look for the 2% that might be true, learn from it and include it.

By using your emotions to inform your decisions and actions early, you can prevent the breakdown of relationships and the build-up of unresolved emotion, which is exhausting.

Appreciation

Teams are more likely to tell each other what they don't want or like. Take time as well to tell people what you appreciate in each other as it deepens the relationships and shows that you witness people and see them as the human being they are.

A Deloitte report titled *The Practical Magic of 'Thank You'* (Vickberg, 2019, p. 23) identified the importance of showing appreciation in a way that engages employees:

> When you recognize someone for their unique contributions to your team or organization, and when you do so in

the way they prefer, it validates them, demonstrates that they belong, and helps them connect with that sense of meaning. At the same time, it can positively impact your work environment, while making the world a better place.

Some people like to be recognised publicly; others prefer a more private thank you email. Learn what motivates different people in your team.

Thank each other for things people do, and equally importantly, thank each other for who you are. By speaking to what you appreciate in someone, you show them they are seen, and you invite them to bring more of their strengths to the team more often. Thank people for what they did and also acknowledge how they did it; for example: 'Thank you for your help with that presentation. I appreciate your attention to detail.'

Alternatively, thank them for what they did and name the impact they had on you personally; for example, 'Thank you for taking the time to work through this problem. You've put my mind at ease, and I know we can work better together when we have future disagreements.' Often at more senior levels, people think appreciation is assumed. We have a fundamental human need to be recognised so nobody is too senior to receive it! It's part of verbalising the non-verbal and is an opportunity for greater connection.

People often dismiss positive feedback, in a form of self-deprecating humility. This is inauthentic humility, born out of the discomfort of receiving praise. If you dismiss positive feedback, you effectively dismiss the opinion of the person giving the feedback. This demonstrates a lack of respect for their opinion and creates disconnection.

Give and receive appreciation to build relationships, to acknowledge each other and motivate each other under pressure. Appreciation can build trust and respect and deepen the relationships in the team.

Inclusive conversations

You won't always agree on everything, so differences of opinion are normal and natural in teamwork.

How do you elevate the quality of your conversation so that everyone has a voice and feels heard and understood?

How do you create space for the challenging conversations to occur – the ones where you voice those differences without attachment to being right or wrong?

How do you create conversation that is explorative and collaborative and builds on each opinion?

How do you listen to what others want from you, without taking it personally?

This is the challenge of teamwork and because it is difficult, it is often avoided, or it is done in a binary 'I'm right, you're wrong' way. Create dialogue where everyone's voice is heard and understood.

Some people talk more than others. Some people think on their feet, join the dots quickly and can articulate a solution to the team. Others need time to reflect, and these people often provide more clarity and greater understanding later after they've had time to do so. The reflectors can often be overlooked as being 'quiet'. Seek to include them in the conversation and explore ways of giving them space to reflect and come back later, especially at times of disagreement. Reflectors may need the information in advance of a meeting or conversation, so they can digest it and come prepared. Ask each other what works best and find ways to meet the needs of everyone in the team. Avoid going with a group consensus and expecting everyone to comply.

Minority groups often have less of a voice because the majority tends to take over. Having a voice and being heard are two different things. If you create space for people to voice their opinions or feelings, it's important not to dismiss those opinions and feelings or ignore them. If someone doesn't feel included and voices it, don't dismiss them, even if you don't agree. Their feelings are valid. It's an opportunity to communicate in a more inclusive way. Conversation needs to include the voice of everyone in the team.

Michelle Obama said: 'Let's invite one another in. Maybe then we can begin to fear less, to make fewer wrong assumptions, to let go of the biases and stereotypes that unnecessarily divide us' (Obama, 2018, p. 421).

Conversation is a two-way process which requires you to listen and seek to understand, for the sake of including the wants and needs of everyone. Don't pretend to listen whilst you wait to have your say. Dialogue requires you to fully understand the other person. If someone repeatedly feels as though they don't have a voice or are not being heard, their frustration levels will rise, and they may become disengaged or disruptive in the team. This will often play out non-verbally and conversation is a great way to explore this.

Fast-paced change often doesn't allow space for conversation, so disagreements go unresolved and unspoken. They create division and become insurmountable over time. Create space in your team to discuss things that are not necessarily directly relevant to your objectives but are relevant and important to the members of the team.

A 2015 McKinsey report titled *Why Diversity Matters* (Hunt, 2015) identified that: 'Companies in the top quartile for racial and ethnic diversity are 35 percent more likely to have financial returns above their respective national industry medians. Companies in the top quartile for gender diversity are 15 percent more likely to have financial returns above their respective national industry medians' (p. 2). The case for diversity has long been understood. And misunderstood.

The Black Lives Matter and the #metoo movements are examples of why we need to create safe spaces for people to have conversations. In 2020, in response to the Black Lives Matter movement, I reached out to my clients and invited them to engage in conversation around race and colour. I felt uncomfortable and unqualified to do so, but if we are to evoke change, we have to step into the zone of uncertainty. A group of us from different businesses and different ethnic backgrounds have convened every month and discussed a variety of topics and instigated a number of different actions in our businesses, communities and professional bodies. It has radically shaped my thinking and vastly expanded my understanding of race and colour. There is much more to do. These conversations are important in every organisation.

Inclusive conversations are uncomfortable so it's easy to avoid them, but the hidden dynamics of those unspoken conversations impact every business. I encourage you to step out of your comfort zone, be curious and create safe spaces for inclusive conversations to develop rapport and understanding. Those conversations will set the tone for how you communicate together in the future and make it easier to resolve differences of opinion based on trust and mutual respect. What is not said often has a greater impact on the team than what is said.

Conversation can reveal the hidden dynamics of your team. Use it to re-align the team using the Organisation Model. You can use the energy and emotions and make sense of them to guide your decisions. Conversation is the foundation for deeper understanding of the team dynamics and actions. In the next three chapters, we will explore other perspectives that create more understanding in the team through Step 3: The Understanding Approach.

 If you'd like to explore this chapter with your own team, download the *OPUS Method of Team Performance* workbook from www.judejennison.com/opus and record your reflections and actions.

Step 3
THE **U**NDERSTANDING APPROACH

In which we explore three levels of awareness to improve decision-making in uncertainty...

Key problems/blind spots

Most teams experience some or all of the following problems and sometimes they may not realise they are happening:

- The team may experience increased stress and polarisation due to uncertainty.
- The team may influence and impact each other unconsciously, either positively or negatively.
- The team may not be aware of or not take advantage of the non-verbal information that guides decision-making.

Hidden dynamics

The three hidden dynamics of the Understanding Approach are:

1. Self-awareness
2. Relational awareness
3. Field awareness

Outcomes

By implementing the Understanding Approach, you will:

- Use the strengths of the team better and reduce polarisation.
- Increase self-awareness and understand the impact of non-verbal behaviour.
- Act confidently and compassionately in the ambiguity and uncertainty of disruptive change.

Chapter 10

SELF-AWARENESS

In which we increase understanding of the impact on self-awareness on the team...

Making an impact

David (not his real name) really cared about his team. He wanted the best for them, so he brought them to work with me. He was concerned that his team were not assertive enough. Standing at 6 feet 4 inches tall and a former rugby player, he had strong energy and a commanding presence. When he briefed me in advance about his team, I saw a gentle, compassionate side too, probably because I was looking for it. I enjoyed meeting him. Having worked in a technology company that had a strong masculine energy, I was comfortable in his presence, and we got on well.

When David and his team came to work with the horses, his team were highly competent. They built strong relationships with the horses, quietly invited them to come with them, and the horses responded well. When David entered the arena with a loose horse, the horse Tiffin took off and careered around the arena. David had gone in with his usual strong energy and had freaked Tiffin out. I asked David to stand quietly in the middle and calm the horse down.

The instant David stood still, Tiffin slowed to a walk. He kept his distance, still unsure of David. David asked Tiffin to walk around the arena at a distance and the two of them built a relationship slowly.

When David came out of the arena, he said: 'I don't know what happened there.'

One of David's team said: 'You have that impact on everyone you meet the first time you meet them.'

Everyone took a sharp intake of breath and took a step back. David looked shocked. It was never his intention, but his strength of energy was causing people to move away for fear of being dominated by him. His team avoided confrontation because they were also intimidated by his presence. David had no idea.

> *Once he realised his energy was naturally strong, he paid attention to how he met people and the impact he had. Several months later, he reported back to say his team were more engaged and more willing to be honest with him.*

Understanding yourself

In Step 2, we explored the art of conversation to raise awareness of the non-verbal behaviours that are happening within the team. In Step 3 of the OPUS Method, we explore this at a deeper level, by looking at three levels of understanding that reveal hidden information to guide your decision-making. The first dynamic in this chapter is to raise awareness of yourself, to understand the impact you have in any given moment and decide what to do about it.

Self-awareness is a crucial skill for leaders and teams. The impact you have on the relationships and the whole team will determine how you collaborate and work together, and therefore the end results. Self-awareness enables a continual fine-tuning in what you do and how you do it, which enables you to refine how you work within a team.

In order to align as a team using the three team roles in Step 1 of this book, self-awareness is critical. If relationships are working and in flow, you can focus on what you are doing. But if a relationship either one-to-one or with the whole team is not in flow, I encourage you to try a different approach. This requires self-awareness. Who you are being has as much impact, if not more, than what you are doing. 'Until you become aware, you aren't acting with any choice guiding your behaviour' (Ekman, 2018).

Use your strengths

Knowing your strengths helps you in moments of struggle. For example, in the midst of conflict, if relationships are a strength of yours, use them! Often people who build strong relationships struggle with conflict because they want harmony. You create harmony by your desire to have it and your ability to work collaboratively through your differences. Whenever something is challenging, reflect on the strengths that you use when it's easy and bring them to the fore.

Consider which of the three team roles work well for you. Do you naturally lead from the front, middle or back? Which one is most comfortable for you, and which one is comfortable for different members of your team? If two of you go into a meeting with a client and both want to lead from the front, you could find yourselves talking over the top of each other, each trying to lead from the front and nobody leading from the side or back to help the client engage with your vision. Don't always default to the same role. Be aware of the role you choose so it is relevant in the moment.

Having awareness of your strengths and how you show up enables you to flex your style into different approaches to get the best out of your team, your clients, suppliers and anyone you interface with. When you know your strengths and the strengths of the team, you can explore the collective strengths. How does your team work together? What do you do brilliantly and where do you get derailed?

Often people will complain about the way their team behave in certain situations. They will blame and criticise others. Having self-awareness means you are aware of what you are doing, as well as what the team as a collective are doing. This gives you information on what needs to be done differently. Sit down with your team and work through the differences and be honest about what is working and what is not, without blame, judgement or criticism.

Intended and unintended impact

Self-awareness is not only about what you do and how you do it. It's important to know your impact.

What impact do you have on the team when you walk into a room?

How do you know?

You are probably aware of everyone else's impact but less aware of your own. Pay attention next time; whether you join a meeting online or in person, you have an impact. What is it?

Are you the one who holds the team accountable (leading from the back)? Or the joker who lightens the mood under pressure (shifting the energy)? Are you the one who continually reminds people of where you are going (leading from the front)? Or draws in the quiet members of the team to ensure their voice is heard (leading from the middle)? Or are you the quiet reflector who misses nothing?

You always have an impact, whether it is intended or not. Most leaders and teams have an impact with little awareness of it. Your impact may be hidden to you, but others are aware of it. When you know your impact, you can flex it and be more conscious about what you want to create.

For example, at a time of pressure in a meeting when the team are struggling, you might want to lighten the mood. You might make a joke about something to create a shift. However, if mistimed, the team may not appreciate the lightness and might be frustrated that you are being flippant. This is an unintended impact. Your intention was to make it easier for the team whereas you were accused of being flippant when it wasn't your intention. We will explore intentions further in Chapter 15.

Notice where you have a positive impact on the mood of the team or on the results that the team create. Notice also where you have a negative impact. 'Without reflection, we go blindly on our way, creating more unintended consequences, and failing to achieve anything useful' (Wheatley, 2002).

Often the person who sees a different perspective will be seen as resistant in a team. Consider how you provide alternative points of view without having the impact of being the person who drags the team down or holds them back. How do you hold a different perspective that has a positive impact in the team and considers the different approaches?

Leaders often have an overinflated view of themselves. We like to think we are doing a good job, so when things don't go well in a team, it's easy to believe you're doing everything right and blame others. Whenever the team are not fully aligned, there is a tendency to look externally at what you want other people to do differently.

Instead, consider the impact you have, and explore what you can do and how you approach things to create that alignment. We are all a work in progress, and there is always room for improvement in how you lead and interact in a team.

Embodied self-awareness

Most people consider self-awareness in the context of *conceptual* self-awareness, which Alan Fogel (2013) describes as 'engagement in a thought process of categorizing, planning, reasoning, judging, and evaluating' (p. 11). Paying attention to your strengths and impact falls into this category.

Rarely do we talk about how our bodies feel, but it is one of the most crucial feedback mechanisms you have. Fogel (2013) describes *embodied* self-awareness as 'the ability to pay attention to ourselves, to feel our sensations, emotions and movement online, in the present moment, without the mediating influence of judgemental thoughts' (p. 1). Embodied self-awareness is critical to the survival of the human species. By having an awareness of our bodies, we can prevent and reduce pain, stop ourselves from bumping into things and manage our physical and emotional health and wellbeing, without having to think about it.

In most industrialised nations, people have been taught to pay more attention to cognitive processing and logical reasoning and have learned to suppress feelings and emotions. This is especially true in the workplace where employees increasingly hold tension in the body, and it becomes so normal that they no longer realise they hold it.

Having awareness of your body informs you on what is happening beyond the words to the relationships and team mood. At times of stress, your body will feel tense. How you feel in your body has an impact on how you show up and therefore has an impact on your team. A stressed tennis player often loses the match, not because they can't serve an ace, but because they can't serve an ace when their body is tense and their mind is frustrated.

Whenever something feels difficult, look for another way of doing things – either by speaking to something that needs to be said, or finding another way. In this way, you find a relaxed state from which to engage with others. This is self-mastery and a continual process of learning and recovering.

Despite how we think we engage with others, we immediately encounter other people as embodied persons, not as objects, machines or physical carriers for their minds. The body provides a gateway to understanding our experience in the world. It provides us with information, not just through seeing, hearing and touch but also through a felt experience that indicates our emotional response to situations. This is valuable information that we typically ignore.

Once you pay more attention to the feedback in your body, you can use any tension to inform you on what needs to happen. It may be an indicator that there are hidden dynamics that need to be revealed through conversation, or it may raise your awareness of the team not being aligned and indicate which of the roles in the Organisation Model need more focus.

You may have learned to ignore tension in your body and regard it as normal. Start using it as a source of information that guides what needs to happen in the team. If you are tense, others in the team will be too. Embodied self-awareness is the gateway to more alignment in the team, better relationships and more harmony.

Where are you holding back?

When you feel confident in a situation or team and there are high levels of trust, you are more likely to show up fully. Trust builds in a team when you are honest about what you think and feel and speak to your wants and needs without judgement. You can feel the strength of this in your body.

By contrast, you are more likely to hold back when you are not sure or when you lack trust, either in yourself or in others. Change creates uncertainty, which often leads to self-doubt. This is exacerbated in a team when disagreements are unresolved, and assumptions have been made. Trust gets eroded and people start to hold back more. Transparent communication is crucial for teams to feel confident about working through differences of opinion.

Polarisation happens at times of uncertainty because we all seek to create clarity where information is missing. In the process, we make judgements based on our values, beliefs, approach and experience. As everyone's experience is different, everyone will have a different point of view about how something should be done. We see how this plays out in the media as people respond to the way governments and organisations behave in a crisis. We often all have a different point of view.

There is a desire to align with those we agree with, and you may be more inclined to spend time with those people. Spending time with those who you disagree with in the team is critical for the whole team to feel connected and engaged together. Be willing to have honest conversations, let go of the negative assumptions you have about others in the team and let go of feeling judged and blamed in return.

Emotional fortitude

Emotion is a normal response to tension. Self-awareness will enable you to manage your emotions and use them as a source of information in interactions, especially where there is tension.

In a Deloitte report, Finzi, Lipton, Lu and Firth (2020, p. 3) describe emotional fortitude as 'the art of examining one's own thoughts and emotions surrounding a decision in order to consider those thoughts and emotions themselves as inputs to the decision-making process'.

They argue that emotions are critical to effective decision making in uncertainty and can be used to generate creativity and further thought. Using emotions and cognitive thinking in balance leads to better decisions, greater trust in the organisation and empowers others. 'When a leader presents an honest assessment of the thoughts and emotions behind a critical decision, others experience and appreciate the leader's authenticity' (p. 6).

Having self-awareness enables you to know your strengths and also identify ways you can stretch. Self-awareness is more than noticing. It's also about taking action. If you know certain relationships need more work, change your approach, notice your impact and try again. In this way, self-awareness becomes a crucial feedback mechanism that enhances how you show up and interact, enabling you to build better relationships and have a more positive influence within a team.

Expand your range

Self-awareness is a foundation for continuous improvement. If you want a high-performing team, self-awareness of every individual and the collective is critical, and that includes embodied self-awareness as well as the awareness of your thought processes. Knowing your impact and the impact of others in the team enables you to continually fine-tune your approach so that you get the best out of each other. When you increase self-awareness, you increase understanding of your emotional responses and can articulate your needs better, leading to a better quality of conversation within the team and greater collaboration.

Be honest with yourself and others, work through differences and communicate transparently to prevent misunderstandings. Know when you are leading from the front, middle or back. Know when it is working and when it is not, and how to switch seamlessly to a different approach when that is needed.

The more self-awareness you have, the greater ability you will have to expand your range of leadership and bring different things to get the best out of the team. In the next chapter, we will build on self-awareness to include awareness of relationships.

 If you'd like to explore this chapter with your own team, download the *OPUS Method of Team Performance* workbook from www.judejennison.com/opus and record your reflections and actions.

Chapter 11

RELATIONAL
AWARENESS

*In which we explore the importance of non-verbal
understanding in relationships...*

Tiffin's story

Tiffin is an ex-racehorse. Born and raced in Ireland, he was sold to someone in England for hunting and sold again every year for four years until he came to me. He was the sweetest horse when he arrived. He did everything I asked for nine months. He was so gentle. He arrived with old whip marks on his face and down his side, so I knew he'd not always had a good experience with humans.

His willingness was learned behaviour to avoid a beating. Once he had learned to express his opinions, he exploded and became aggressive, physically using his 700kg of weight to shove me around. He'd only ever been compliant to avoid being the victim. When he realised that he didn't need to be a victim, he became the aggressor. He had no idea how to be in a relationship based on trust and respect.

I gave him six months off work, and then I put him on a return-to-work programme. He took two years to learn to trust again. I had mistaken Tiffin's compliance for willingness when in fact it was a mask for fear. Fear of having a voice, fear of getting it wrong in case he took another beating. Fear of articulating his needs, fear of change and therefore tolerating everything that was expected until he could tolerate no more.

This is just like millions of people in organisations. When I tell clients his story, they often express their horror at how anyone could beat a horse. But we emotionally beat people down in organisations every day. And the difference between compliance and willingness is so subtle, it's almost impossible to read.

Several years on and Tiffin is extremely confident, but he remains highly sensitive to anxiety in clients because he associates anxiety and stress with him being badly treated. He senses how people feel and will move away from stress and anxiety.

Self and relationships

All relationships are different, and they impact how you show up and therefore the impact you have. You will be different in a relationship with a father, daughter, partner, friends, siblings, colleagues, customers and suppliers. Not because you are inauthentic, but because the relationship itself requires different aspects of you. The common theme in the relationship is authenticity but how authentic are you really? Just as Tiffin was afraid to show up fully, people in teams hide behind the mask of who they think they should be, especially when there are differences of opinion, and this creates distance.

Not all about you

Whilst self-awareness is crucial, the world is not spinning around your axis. Therefore, increasing awareness of the relationships and paying attention to how others respond to you and the relationship will enable you to stretch into different aspects of your leadership to ensure that you get the best out of the relationships.

Relationships are where teams often break down so developing the skill of relational awareness is crucial to team success. Peter F. Drucker famously said in an interview with Bill Moyers: 'The most important thing in communication is to hear what isn't being said' (Moyers, 1989, p. 408).

Pay attention to how others respond to you. Who is engaged, and who is disengaged? Who do you connect with easily and who do you find more challenging? Where is there disagreement and polarisation? Where is there anxiety or stress? All of these are felt in the relationship without needing to be spoken to. How do you show up differently in different situations?

The tendency will be to move away from dissonance and towards resonance. That's why relationships tend to spiral upwards or downwards, and polarisation rarely gets resolved. Having a more conscious approach to the relationship will provide you with new information and can deepen the connection, particularly with those who you disagree with. This becomes even more critical in a team because one broken relationship can derail a whole team and waste energy.

Reflect on what you think and feel about people, notice where you get tension in your body when there is discord or stress. Notice how that builds in relationship with particular people and lessens with others. Tension in your body is a reminder that there is something that needs to be spoken to or resolved. A greater level of trust or a conversation to understand polarised views may be needed.

At the heart of great leadership, teamwork and relationships is a better quality of listening. With relational awareness, listen to what is not being said, as much as what is being said.

Notice where you are aligned and where you are not. What happens in your body to inform you? What can you do differently that may result in a different response?

Power with, not over

The word 'power' is uncomfortable for many people because it tends to be regarded as a negative thing. Power is often confused with 'power over'. I want you to consider power as 'power with' instead. This is an equal relationship.

Relationships are either based on 'power over' or 'power with'. If there is 'power over', one person will have ultimate control. You may give away power to a more senior leader, senior officials, sometimes to clients and people who you regard as more experienced or more knowledgeable. In this way, you allow them to call the shots and have the final say.

Louise (name changed) is a people pleaser. She spends ages building a relationship with a horse, talking to it, stroking it on the neck. Out of a desire to be kind, compassionate and relational, she doesn't want to ask the horse to do anything the horse doesn't want to do.

The horse connects and turns towards her. Louise looks at me and asks why the horse is not moving. 'Where are you going?' I ask, and she says: 'Oh, I don't know. I was waiting for the horse to move and decide where to go.'

The horse has made a decision. They are not moving. In the absence of clarity and direction from Louise, the horse has decided not to move.

When people first work with my horses, many people give away their power. They realise that they've met their physical match, and that they will never win in a tug of war with a horse. Instead, they go too far the other way, and in a desire not to be too forceful, they give away their power and become passive, like Louise did. This is a 'power over' relationship where you give your power away to the other party. In the desire to make the relationship important, you become passive and don't have a voice.

By contrast, Steve (name changed) approaches the horse, and without saying hello or stroking the horse or building a relationship in any way, he demands 'Right, move. We are going.'

Steve heads off, and the horse will either stand still and refuse to engage, or headbutt him and engage in a power struggle. There is no relationship.

Steve is so focused on where he wants to go that he forgets to build the relationship and invite the horse to come with him. He never considers that the horse might not want to.

This is the opposite form of 'power over' relationship where Steve tries to take all the power and be in control. This may be a subconscious decision, but it has an impact. People will respond to control in two ways. Either they will resist your control, or they will acquiesce.

These are the two extremes that occur when you focus purely on the result or on the relationship. Neither approach is effective, and there is an imbalance of respect. This is why teams often break down. Steve is using 'power over' to get his own way and Louise is left feeling as though she doesn't have a voice or is not valued.

Whilst Steve's approach may work short term with someone more dominant than Louise, he needs to flex his style with her to encourage her and make space for her to have a voice. Louise may find she has a voice with people who are quieter and less assertive than Steve, but she needs to claim her space and make her needs clear.

Both blame the other, which leads to both not changing their behaviour, and so the problem continues. If either of them modified their behaviour and matched the other in energy, their relationship would improve. If both modified their behaviour, they could transform their relationship with greater honesty, clarity, trust and respect. Both could fine-tune and find a more balanced way of leading, without control and without being controlled.

Both types of 'power over' relationships are out of balance and unequal. Many people will tell me that due to a hierarchy in the organisation, relationships are not equal. Whilst the job title and levels of responsibility and authority may not be equal, your leadership ability and energy can be. By diminishing yourself or others, you cease to get the best from the relationship and do not allow for collaboration, creativity and innovation.

True collaboration and therefore 'power with' comes from everyone having an equal say and feeling safe to express their opinion. Before you even speak, sense the relationship. Make sure you embody the 'power with' approach, neither giving away or taking too much power. Read the energy of others, match them in their energy, and work with them to create a result.

A different perspective

In a team, it is easy to get fixated on the ultimate objectives and forget about the relationships. How well do you understand the people in your team? Do you know their values, beliefs and opinions? They may differ from yours, and you may need to consider how you bridge those divides. You won't change someone else's values any more than they will change yours, but by having a common understanding on where you are aligned and where you differ, you can work more collaboratively together.

Your values and those of your team influence how you act and behave. Pay attention to what is not being said and use your knowledge of your team to guide decisions. Be careful not to make assumptions about what you think is happening in the relationship. We will cover this in more detail in Chapter 14 on assumptions.

Relationships provide different perspectives that are useful in a team. For example, if you are someone who looks at the bigger picture, don't get frustrated with the people in the team who pay attention to the detail. Both are needed at different times. Instead, consider how you use the different strengths of the individuals in the team to ensure that both the big picture and the detail are considered appropriately. Build on the strengths of each other and respect those differences as valuable.

We read relationships unconsciously, and often you may spend more time with those in the team who you agree with and less time with those who you disagree with. In this way, you deepen some relationships and cause greater divides in others. This is noticeable in a team and everyone will feel it. Notice where you create distance and make an effort to bridge divides, so the team stay aligned.

Non-transactional communication

When teams are busy, as most teams are, there is a tendency to communicate transactionally and operationally – to gather and impart information when it is needed. Many team meetings become information gathering rather than collaborative sessions. People switch off when someone else is talking because it is of little interest to them. This is how many teams operate – as a group of individuals and not as a collaborative team working together.

Pay attention to the relationships in the team. Consider who is struggling, not by what is being said, but by what is not being said. How might you support them? Where there are disagreements, they will continue to exist until you work through them. Use the dissonance as an invitation to be curious and find ways to work together to meet the needs of everyone and find full alignment.

Take time to get to know the people who you interact with least in the team. Until you feel comfortable in the presence of everyone and fully free to speak to what you need, trust is missing and will impact the whole team. By building stronger relationships, you minimise wrong assumptions, increase trust and build stronger allies and support.

You may think you are too busy to spend time building relationships. You are too busy not to. The relationships in the team, and the strength of them, will determine the success of your team. Take time to build strong relationships with everyone, and the results will come faster.

Strengthen relationships

Relationships are the tricky part of working in a team because there will always be differences of opinion. It often starts at the non-verbal level of sensing and feeling the differences. Assumptions get made, trust is lessened, and dissonance and distance are created. When you have a more conscious awareness of what is happening in relationships, you can address them before ingrained patterns of avoidance or heated debate are created.

People often ask me how they can handle the 'difficult' person in their team. Other people in the team are not the problem, just as you are not the problem person either. The relationship is the problem, and you are a part of creating that relationship. Every member of the team has a responsibility to resolve team problems, and that starts by strengthening the relationships in the team, so that everyone feels safe to have the necessary conversations to speak to differences and bridge the divides. Be open and willing to change your point of view for the benefit of the team.

Relationships are created through conversations, through support, a willingness to face into the disagreements and explore how you meet the needs of everyone. Use the available non-verbal feedback as a starting point to create greater connection rather than distance, and the team will strengthen and resolve problems together.

 If you'd like to explore this chapter with your own team, download the *OPUS Method of Team Performance* workbook from www.judejennison.com/opus and record your reflections and actions.

Chapter 12

FIELD AWARENESS

In which we expand awareness of additional non-verbal information...

Panic gets you nowhere

I was apprehensive on arrival as I had little experience with horses. As I walked through the car park, I saw the horses watching me from a field separated by a gate; they were bigger than I thought they would be and I swear they were trying to get a read on me, as I was with them.

After an initial introduction to the horses, we moved to an exercise around giving direction with confidence and using non-verbal cues to develop trust. One by one we walked one of the horses around the paddock ring. Leading a horse is much more difficult than you think and definitely more difficult than handing out actions in a morning buzz. My turn quickly arrived. I approached the horse Kalle with confidence and a certain apprehension. I introduced myself to her and invited her to come with me. After some initial reluctance, she moved. My heart was racing, but I was pleased that she was cooperating. I talked to her as we walked, and my confidence built as we went.

We were halfway around the circuit when something caught my eye. A dot in the sky was moving very quickly: I thought it was a plane at first; it was a plane, but it was a low-flying military jet. PANIC! My experience in work has taught me that my panic is contagious and non-productive; decisive action was required. I was too far away from everyone to make it back. I was not going to leave the horse, so my only option was to stay put and work through the situation.

We stopped; I looked Kalle in the eye and said, 'It is going to be ok.' I talked to Kalle and stroked the side of her head to reassure her. The jet screamed overhead, my legs were shaking, and Kalle looked concerned but stayed with me. I walked back to the group. Kalle moved straight away this time; we had built trust based on our shared experience.

> *Here is what I learned from this experience:*
>
> - *I can go into an unfamiliar situation and be confident and trust my instincts.*
> - *Stay calm under pressure. Ignoring risks or hitting the panic button will put you in a bad place.*
> - *Caring for those that you work with builds trust.*
> - *Trying something new can be surprising and teach you more than you thought it would.*
>
> Ross Easterby, Data Governance Manager, Wesleyan

What's happening out there?

I often hear people say: 'It just came out of nowhere.' Whilst this can happen, often people are focused on the detail of what they are doing or are so absorbed in the relationship that they lose sight of the bigger picture and don't realise that things are changing around them. Despite being extremely anxious, Ross was aware of his own fear (self-awareness), looking after Kalle (relational awareness) and also was aware of the plane (field awareness). This helped him make decisions that kept us all safe. I had also spotted the plane before Ross and was ready to take over if I needed to.

Paying attention to the wider field provides clarity, direction and information at times of change and uncertainty. This information can guide your decision-making and ensure you make decisions that benefit the wider picture, beyond your team. The more you pay attention to the field, the quicker you can react and minimise the impact of being surprised by an apparent sudden turn of events.

Whilst the relationships are the foundation within the team, it is important to consider the team as a single entity and to pay

OPUS

attention to it as a whole as well as the component parts. Consider the team as the bigger picture and the relationships within it as the component parts.

Often people get drawn into the individual relationships, or the thing they are currently focused on, and lose sight of the bigger picture. How aware are you of what is happening in other parts of the business, and what are you doing to ensure that the whole team is successful?

How aware are you of the bigger picture outside of your immediate team, and how does that inform you as it changes constantly? Does your team stay focused on the direction, or get lost in the detail?

What is field awareness?

A team is a system. When your attention is on one person or thing, there are always other people and things that need to be taken into account. If you focus all your attention on product development, you may lose sight of the customer experience. If you focus on sales, the quality of delivery may slip. This is why there is always tension within a business between sales, delivery and product development. They need to be considered within the context of the whole, as an ecosystem, rather than the sum of the parts.

Field awareness starts by paying attention at the team level, but it goes much further. Your customers, suppliers, the economy, market conditions, the political system, government regulations, health and safety all have an impact on your business, and therefore awareness needs to be expanded to include them all. The team may also have their own personal challenges that impact their mood, energy levels and focus.

There is a wealth of information that can guide what you do next. In uncertainty, people seek clarity and direction when often there appears not to be any. The wider field can guide you on what is needed.

For example, when the Covid-19 pandemic caused the UK to go into lockdown in 2020, my work with horses stopped instantly and therefore my income.

My self-awareness was: I need to generate income to fund my horses and keep them alive, as well as keep my business afloat.

My field awareness was: There is a mood of anxiety in the country associated with the uncertainty.

My relational awareness was: If the general mood in the country is one of anxiety, my clients may be struggling too. I called clients and discovered that many of their teams were struggling with the uncertainty of the situation. I offered them online sessions for their teams to discuss how they were responding to the uncertainty and share my learning from my previous book, *Leading Through Uncertainty*.

The solution was informed by my needs, the mood of the country and the needs of my clients. I might not have developed the idea sat at home on my own but recognising the mood in the country and engaging my clients enabled me to pivot my business in the first week of lockdown and save the lives of my horses by generating income in a new way. I created a solution that met the needs of all parties, informed initially by the field.

Most of the world's problems are already known. At some point there will be a major cybersecurity attack. How resilient and secure is your IT? The World Economic Forum *Global Risks Report* 2019 (Collins, 2019) highlights many of the issues that we stick our heads in the sand and ignore. By being better prepared, we position ourselves to respond more quickly.

What's happening in the field?

The mood of your team will be determined by many factors: their health, financial position, how engaged they are with the work, whether it fits their values, their personal challenges at home – moving house, looking after children or ageing parents, divorce and much more. All of these things affect how your team perform. You won't always know what is happening in the wider field, but you will sense the change in people as their circumstances change.

That's why it's important to create an environment of trust and psychological safety so the team feels safe sharing what is happening, as much as they want to, and as far as it impacts their work.

What is happening in your team? Who are the quiet ones whose voices need bringing in? How do you know when someone is reflecting versus disengaged? What do you need to pay attention to? What resistance needs to be addressed? Who needs time to reflect? Who is close to burnout and needs pressure taking off them?

A team is fluid, ever-changing. If one person changes, the whole team changes. If one relationship is difficult, the whole team is affected. It has a knock-on effect on your customers too. They will sense when your team is enthusiastic, engaged and in harmony. They will also sense dissonance, disagreements and discord.

What happens in the team is sensed by the wider field as much as you sense the wider field. Otto Scharmer and Katrin Kaufer describe this as *eco-system awareness*. 'It requires people to develop the capacity to perceive problems from the perspectives of others. The result is decisions and outcomes that benefit the whole system, not just a part of it' (Scharmer and Kaufer, 2013, p. 57).

You know when something is happening with a client by how they engage with you. When they create distance, it means something. It could mean that they are disengaging from you personally or from your business, perhaps because they no longer want your service, or it no longer meets their needs. Or it could mean that they are making changes in their business that they have not yet shared with you.

Those changes might impact you; they might not. Paying attention in this way requires you to slow down, reflect on what is happening, and decide how you respond in order to meet the needs of everyone. Consider when to follow up and when the client might need space.

What does everyone want and need?

How well do you know what your team think and feel about different things? As teams get to know each other, they start to rely on default patterns of behaviour as the norm and assumptions start to increase. This deepens trust or creates divisions. Therefore, the relationships that start off well will probably continue to grow, whereas the ones where there are disagreements continue to divide unless corrective action is taken.

Often people will test their ideas and assumptions on the people who are most likely to agree with them. Instead, test your assumptions and ideas out on the people in the team who are least likely to agree. By doing this, you gain an alternative perspective early on in the ideas process, but you also provide an opportunity to demonstrate that you value the opinions of the people who may not agree with you. This increases trust and respect within the team and improves the way you work together as a whole unit, rather than relying on pockets of relationships that work and avoiding the ones that don't.

Remember that your needs change as circumstances change, and so will the needs of others. Therefore, continuous communication and clarity are needed at times of change. Often during change, there is a lack of clarity as you re-establish the priorities. Ambiguity and uncertainty make people uncomfortable. Field awareness requires you to pay attention to the changing needs of the teams, as well as the relationships and your own self-awareness. Each builds on the other.

Whenever there is tension, we feel it before anyone speaks to it. By paying attention to the wider field, you can look for the needs and wants of others and make decisions based on how to meet them. Reflect on whose needs are not being met in the team. Who is not aligned? What needs to happen?

By paying attention to the wider field, you pre-empt problems that may arise later before they become a major crisis. For example, early tension in a team can be resolved quickly by discussing the root cause of the tension. This prevents frustration from building in the team, minimises further misunderstandings and reduces the disruption of a breakdown in relationships.

Field awareness is a proactive way of seeking information, often non-verbally, before you need it and can prevent issues from arising or escalating out of proportion. It relies on having collaborative and explorative conversations as described in Chapter 9.

Market conditions

Market conditions are another form of field awareness that influences your team, what you do and how you do it. Pay attention to your customers. What do they want and need? How do their needs change according to market conditions? For example, if your major client's customers are struggling, they may reduce their budgets, which will reduce revenue for your client and therefore could have an impact on what they need from you. By working with them early on, you will understand their needs and be able to respond quickly.

It may require you to modify your products and services to meet their needs. For example, as more jobs are replaced by artificial intelligence, recruitment companies will need to consider how they do business. What type of roles are they focusing on and which ones are likely to be redundant in the future? A recruitment company could be proactive and identify re-training opportunities for their clients who are in a particular industry that is likely to be affected. In this way, they provide additional value and divert services to a new area of need.

Pay attention to your suppliers. Are there issues that need resolving? Has a major contact within a supplier changed, and what impact is that having? How do you ensure that it does not erode the service or quality of the products they provide to you? And what do you need to do in advance to prevent that from happening?

Often teams do not pay enough attention to their suppliers, and they wait until the relationship degrades and then move to a new one. This is time-consuming for both parties. It's far better to resolve issues early on, as you would in your own team.

In addition, pay attention to the wider market conditions. The Brexit vote took many people by surprise, yet the signs of polarisation within the country were already there. Don't allow your team to be surprised by changes in market conditions. Try to be one step ahead, and keep your whole team abreast of what you are seeing and noticing in the wider field.

We have commonly heard that the whole is greater than the sum of its parts; however, we tend to consider a team as the whole. The whole should include the wider field of awareness to ensure that you factor in all of the available information.

Multi-awareness

You may believe that you lack clarity in the uncertainty of change, but there is a wealth of information to guide decision-making. By paying attention to the field, as well as self and relationships, you will be more well-rounded and holistic in your thinking.

Use the available information to guide you in uncertainty. Switch your focus continually from self to relationships to field and cycle round all three continuously, building on the information as you discover it. There are few surprises when we pay attention at the field level.

In the next and final step, Step 4: The Stories Blueprint, we will dig deeper into the hidden stories that everyone creates and explore how they show up in the field.

If you'd like to explore this chapter with your own team, download the *OPUS Method of Team Performance* workbook from www.judejennison.com/opus and record your reflections and actions.

Step 4
THE **S**TORIES BLUEPRINT

In which we explore the unconscious stories that make, or break, teamwork…

Key problems/blind spots

Most teams experience some or all of the following problems and sometimes they may not realise these are happening:

- The team make assumptions and judgements about people and situations and act as though they are true.
- The team may create distance, dissonance and division unconsciously.
- The team may erode trust and mutual respect when there are differences of opinion.

Hidden dynamics

The hidden dynamics of the Stories Blueprint are:

1. Boundaries
2. Assumptions
3. Intentions

Outcomes

By implementing the Stories Blueprint, you will:

- Have clear boundaries and hold them with compassion and clarity.
- Increase openness, honesty and transparency in the team by articulating assumptions without blame, judgement and criticism.
- Act with clear intentions that get positive results and have a positive influence on others.

Chapter 13

BOUNDARIES

In which we learn how boundaries are an act of compassion....

Understanding my boundaries

When I started my journey with Jude on a cold, winter February morning, I became aware that previous personal and traumatic experience had hardened my usually soft centre. Inner turmoil caused my judgement to be misplaced. My inner voice said I was wrong all the time; I questioned each decision I made and every challenge from others. I was enforcing a one-size-fits-all boundary that was not useful, not authentic and should only be reserved for one person in the past.

I remember the exact moment that I realised this. I was attempting to guide a horse called Tiffin through an obstacle course in the arena. We started off 'ok', but as soon as we got to the first bend he stopped and refused to move any further. I tried everything to no avail. Jude could see I was struggling and came over to offer support – she said, 'Do you always doubt yourself when you are challenged?' and that was it for me. The pivotal moment in my life where the penny dropped and I knew that the only person that could change me is, well, me.

Understanding my own boundaries has without doubt been my biggest learning during this life-changing journey. Jude (and her horses) showed me how to hold these at my core; to allow the authentic me to be present. But it is equally as important to know when to really stand firm and when to soften, to know how and when to let go, and to know it will be ok whatever the outcome, good or bad.

I am now more mindful of what I can and can't control and trust my own instinct. I take each situation or challenge individually; and know that as long as I trust my core values (which I hold close to my heart) and remain authentic to who I am, the outcome will be fine. Through the time spent with Jude and the horses, I have become confident in who I am, to have

> *the courage and conviction in my decision-making; to really know and understand myself and stay strong.*
>
> *When you are facing yourself with the horses, you can't hide. They see you; they feel you; they know.*
>
> Sarah Frost, Resource Manager, Entec Si

What are boundaries?

Boundaries are the guidelines for how you live and work. They provide the limits and rules you set in your relationships, and therefore within your team. They provide the guidance for what you say yes to and what you say no to. Parents create boundaries for children to keep them safe; for example, you probably wouldn't let your four-year-old walk to the shop on their own. At what age would you deem it to be safe? That would depend on your personal experience, the area you live, how busy the roads are, whether the child is going with an older sibling or completely alone, how sensible your child has proved to be with previous responsibilities given.

Children continually push against boundaries as they grow and develop. This is common and healthy. Yet as adults, boundaries often become more rigid or non-existent. If you've worked for a controlling boss, you might not want to work for another one. You might say no to the job as a way of managing your boundary, or you might have learned to have the skills to deal with someone who is controlling and therefore be more willing to take the job.

There are no binary answers with boundaries. They are contextual (based on the person, relationship and situation), and they are constantly changing. Each person in the team will often unconsciously set their own boundaries and each person will set them differently. Therefore, it's important to understand what is and isn't ok in a team. What is ok in one relationship is not ok in another. What is ok in one team with one set of people is not ok in another.

These are decisions that we all have to make, and they depend on the levels of trust and respect you have, as well as your own self-confidence, self-belief, self-awareness and previous experience. As you can imagine, this is a minefield when working in a team, as most people are unconsciously setting boundaries, managing them, ignoring them, stepping over them and challenging them!

It is crucial for teams to develop the ability to speak openly and honestly about boundaries without judgement. The Pillars of Vitality provide insight and guidance for managing boundaries. Having healthy boundaries improves wellbeing and reduces stress. Notice how your energy is impacted by boundaries that are challenged or pushed against. It can create an energy of resistance, increase frustration and you will feel the impact of this in your body. A team who communicates their boundaries openly will understand each other better. They increase levels of trust and mutual respect by knowing when to challenge, when to support and when to hold back. Authentically.

Not holding boundaries

If you don't manage your boundaries, you may find yourself being pushed around by others. Most people will have times when they accept something that someone says or does, even though they don't like it. Most office banter steps over the boundaries of compassion for others. If you engage in the banter and make fun of yourself (or others), you may be engaging in office banter to be liked and to belong. This is an example of not holding boundaries.

If you don't have clear boundaries, you may find yourself doing things you don't want to do, going along with team decisions that you disagree with and not having a voice. Or you may think you've expressed your opinion, but nobody listens, and you get carried along even though you don't like it. If your boundary continues to be stepped over, even when you've voiced it, it's up to you to reinforce it by being clear about what is not ok for you and what you want instead.

If you always say yes to everyone to keep them happy, you may have boundaries that are too flexible. In a team, this is rife with hidden consequences. The person in the team who always says yes will often have a higher workload, may be under more pressure and may feel constantly stressed. They may feel put upon, pushed around and frustrated, but they daren't say no. The frustration and stress levels will continue to rise until you say no and hold a clear boundary.

If you have unhealthy boundaries that are not held, you may also find yourself oversharing, constantly trying to justify yourself, or feeling anxious about what everyone else thinks. In the absence of you setting clear boundaries, your team will either trample all over them or walk on eggshells as they try to work out where the boundaries should be for you. And they will falsely assume, all the time.

All of this is hidden, often unconscious, but continuously played out in a team, and it uses up huge amounts of energy as everyone tries to second guess what everyone else wants, as well as themselves. If frustration is building in a team, there is a good chance that boundaries have been stepped over and not challenged, and someone is putting up with something that is not ok for them.

Another example is behaviour that you tolerate and don't like but never speak to. This is common in teams. For example, there may be one person who is always late to meetings and everyone may sit around waiting for them. If that is ok and you enjoy five minutes of connection without the final team member, then there is no problem. However, if you find yourselves getting irritated because one person always does something you don't like, it is important to speak to it.

Often teams will ignore having honest conversations around boundaries because it feels uncomfortable, so the frustration continues. If you want people to like you, you may discover that you don't set clear boundaries and find yourself pushed around or tolerating things you don't want. It's important to create dialogue around boundaries to prevent disconnection, or a breakdown in trust and respect.

Rigid boundaries

Conversely, if you hold too rigid a boundary, you may create distance between yourself and the team, either physically, mentally, emotionally or socially. Often people hold too rigid a boundary because they fear being pushed around so they go too far the other way and become fixed in their opinions and approaches. If you fear being pushed around or you think someone is trying to hurt you, you may hold a rigid boundary as a way of protecting yourself. This often shows up as being disconnected, disengaged or unwilling in a team. If you hold people at a distance, don't ask for help or don't share openly with others, you may be holding rigid boundaries as a form of self-protection.

If you hold the belief that you are vastly different at work to how you are at home, you are not being authentic and are holding rigid boundaries as a form of self-protection. This keeps the team at a distance and prevents trust and openness. It is important to continually challenge your own sense of what feels right so you continue to stretch.

If you find yourself judging someone as 'stubborn' (or you are being judged as stubborn by others), it is probably because they are holding a strong boundary to keep themselves safe. Instead of pushing against the boundary, be curious about what their need is and why they need to hold the boundary so strongly. By having an open and curious conversation, you deepen understanding of each other and find ways to support each other as you work towards common objectives and deepen the levels of trust.

You have to push against your own boundaries to learn and develop. Stepping out of your comfort zone requires you to challenge your own boundary of what might feel comfortable. If you are uncomfortable stepping out of your comfort zone, you probably hold rigid boundaries and may be seen to be inflexible by the rest of the team. This will make it harder for you to work in a team where flexibility is crucial for everyone to work together. If you avoid learning, doing something new or stepping out of your comfort zone, practise doing things differently and gradually develop the skill of stretching your boundaries and comfort zone. Support others in your team to do so too.

Boundaries are continually changing and it's difficult to know where the line is drawn. If you step over a boundary, it feels uncomfortable, and so does being out of the comfort zone. How do you know when to stretch and when to say no? It's a continual process of trial and error. When working in a team, you need to develop the skill of knowing what feels right in any given moment and be willing to stretch enough but not too much that it feels wrong for you.

Healthy boundaries

Boundaries are an act of self-compassion and self-respect. If you have healthy boundaries, you respect yourself enough to feel comfortable saying no to things that are not ok for you. It leads to an open and honest conversation. In the process, you create understanding about what is ok and what is not ok, even if you still disagree.

Self-awareness and embodied self-awareness are critical foundations for recognising when your boundaries are being challenged because usually you will sense it in your body. It will feel uncomfortable in some way. The more awareness you develop in your body, the more you will know the difference between the discomfort of stepping out of your comfort zone and the discomfort of a boundary being challenged. Each person in the team has to find their own experience of this, just as when you learn to ride a bike, you find your balance without having the words for it. It is an embodied experience.

Healthy boundaries enable you to hold compassion for others without being sucked into their drama. It's important to hold boundaries with compassion for others, without blame, judgement or criticism, trusting that everyone is doing their best in any given moment.

Setting and holding boundaries is always a balance. Do you say no to the workload and risk losing out on a promotion, or do you say yes to going the extra mile and working longer hours in order to get the promotion? Only you can answer that as you have to weigh up the risk, the discomfort and the reward and make a decision accordingly. It will be different for everyone.

We make decisions on our boundaries on a daily basis, but mostly we go about our work and life without being aware of those decisions. By being more conscious of what you say yes to and what you say no to (and the associated consequences and impact of each), you can make powerful choices that benefit both you and your team, and help you stay focused on where you are going together.

Holding your boundaries

Having healthy boundaries creates vitality in the team. Having more open and honest conversations about boundaries in your team enables you to support, guide and challenge each other in setting and holding those boundaries. If you don't speak openly about your boundaries within the team, or it does not feel psychologically safe to do so, you will make more assumptions about each other and the team. This will create further distance, disconnection and misunderstandings. We will explore the impact of assumptions in the next chapter.

Be honest, open and clear about your boundaries and articulate what you want, as well as what you don't want. This provides guidance for others on how to handle the situation and provides a clear expectation. When you articulate a boundary that has been stepped over, you ask the other person to change their behaviour. Recognise that they may forget, and you may need to re-articulate the boundary. Avoid being frustrated by mistakes and continue to re-emphasise what is ok and what is not ok. Make sure you are flexible in return whilst holding your boundary.

By opening the dialogue around boundaries, you create an opportunity to deepen relationships, connect and understand each other better. If you avoid the conversation, the impact will be increasing frustration and an imbalance of power with some people feeling pushed around and others feeling as though they call all the shots.

Boundaries enable more creativity in the team as you flex more within known guidelines, trusting that people will speak honestly about their frustrations without blame, judgement or criticism. Boundaries are important and healthy. The more you reveal the hidden dynamics of boundaries in your team, the more you develop trust and mutual respect and can speak openly to areas of disagreement without taking it personally.

 If you'd like to explore this chapter with your own team, download the *OPUS Method of Team Performance* workbook from www.judejennison.com/opus and record your reflections and actions.

Chapter 14

ASSUMPTIONS

In which we let go of self-talk and negativity in favour of conversation and transparency...

The stubborn one

> *'I'll work with one of the other horses because Kalle looks aloof.'*
> *'I don't think she likes me because she's the only horse who has not come and said hello to me.'*
> *'This horse doesn't want to work.'*
> *'Is this horse the stubborn one?'*

These are comments I regularly hear from clients about my horse Kalle. In fact, Kalle is very interested in building a relationship. She's not at all aloof but she is very self-assured, which people often find intimidating because of her sheer size. When people hold back and are afraid to approach her, she responds by not wanting to engage with them in return. It's because Kalle is so self-assured that she refuses to engage with anything less than your authentic self. If you give your power away, she won't engage. She wants you to bring yourself fully into the relationship.

Clients often describe the horses as stubborn or difficult when the horses refuse to engage or cooperate. My response is: 'You've not yet met the conditions for them to want to engage.' When a person's behaviour appears challenging, there is a tendency to judge them. It's easy to blame others because you avoid having to change your own behaviour.

With my team, both horse and human, I consider all behaviour as feedback that informs how I interact with them. If I'm not getting the result that I want, it is my responsibility to change my approach. Instead of making negative assumptions, I assume they want something different from my leadership. By changing my behaviour, I change the behaviour of others.

When the horses are soft and gentle, it's usually because I am relaxed and calm. I've learned to manage my energy in an authentic way so that I am settled in my body and relaxed. On a windy day, I may need to draw on this energy more to help the horses feel calm, so they trust me to keep them safe. I'm never complacent with them.

When the horses are challenging, there is always an unmet need. When they jostle at the gate on a wet and windy day, it's usually because they want to come in for a feed to get warm. If I turned up late in the morning, Opus used to rear up at the gate. He was ready for his breakfast, and he made it clear. Does that make him difficult? No. It made him clear. I learned that if I arrived before 9am, he was happy, and if I was later, he wasn't. I could still choose what time I arrived, but I made my decision consciously knowing what he wanted, as well as what I wanted.

In this way, you can use feedback to guide you in your interactions, to continually seek to create conditions that make others thrive, as well as meeting your own needs for being relaxed and content. It involves continual conversation to avoid making false assumptions that break relationships.

Task-based assumptions

An assumption is defined in the *Oxford English Dictionary* as 'acceptance that something is true without having proof'.

In the desire to create clarity, we make assumptions about people and situations. Some of these assumptions make our lives easier; others cause division in relationships. Assumptions speed up the process. You assume your alarm clock will go off at the time you set it. This kind of assumption reduces your stress. You won't lie awake all night worrying whether your alarm will go off. You assume it will because there is no reason for it not to.

In the desire to ease the uncertainty of task-based activities with others, we make assumptions about people too. For example, it would be reasonable to assume that a newer or less experienced member of a team may need more detailed instructions, whereas a more experienced team member will need less. This will be based on your experience of working with that person.

151

Imagine you want your team to build a chair. If you ask them to build a chair, they may build an armchair, but you might want an office chair. Do you want wheels on it? What fabric is it made of? An experienced team member might know that you only ever ask for an office chair, so they make assumptions that speed up the process, and you make assumptions that they know what you want without needing to be given all the detail. Asking for a chair would be enough with someone who worked with you regularly.

Practical assumptions speed up decisions, actions and inter-actions within the team. You don't need to spell everything out in detail every time. Consider where assumptions in your team speed up the process.

Assumptions also derail teams if they turn out not to be true. If you assumed that someone knew what you wanted and they didn't, they might waste time doing a piece of work that is not what is needed. Continually creating mutual understanding is therefore critical for efficiency.

If you've never asked your team to build a chair before, they may make incorrect assumptions. You might need to provide more information the first time something is done if you have an idea in your head or a vision of how you think it should be. Test your assumptions with the team and make sure there is clarity on what is expected. This will enable you to stay out of the detail of the execution and instead allow for regular updates from the middle instead. Therefore, making assumptions about tasks is more productive and efficient as long as expectations are clear and understood and communication is continuous.

Relationship-based assumptions

In relationships, assumptions are one of the most common forms of non-verbal awareness that you may have. You make assumptions about who in your team will agree, who will be difficult and who will disagree. Your assumptions determine your energy and behaviour towards the relationships and have an impact on those people. In the same way, those people make assumptions about you and your energy. Assumptions create a continual non-verbal conversation between people and lead to more trust or less trust depending on whether your assumptions are positive or negative.

Assumptions are rife at times of conflict or disagreement. If you've had a disagreement with someone, it's common to assume that they will continue to disagree, or you may judge them to be difficult. This affects how open you might be and therefore the levels of trust you have. The next time you meet this person, you will show up based on your assumptions about them. People will sense this in each other's energy and respond accordingly. If you show up with your guard up because you assume there might be conflict, the other person will match you in that same energy. In this way, it's easy to create a spiral of mistrust based on an assumption that may not be true.

How you show up has an impact, and assumptions influence this enormously without you realising it. The more conscious you are about the assumptions you make, the more you can choose to drop that assumption in favour of something that might improve the relationship rather than cause it to break down further.

If you assume that someone is pushing your boundaries to annoy you, you break trust and create distance. People rarely push boundaries to irritate you. They push boundaries by mistake without realising it. If you've not had clear conversations around your boundaries within your team or your relationships, then it's easy to make assumptions and act on them, discovering later that you broke down trust as a result of misreading the situation or person.

Trust that when someone steps over your boundary, it is often done unconsciously and by mistake. Don't assume that they want to do you harm. Otherwise, you will go round holding rigid boundaries as self-protection. If you assume that everyone is doing their best, you can work with mistakes and speak to them openly.

Assume that everyone gets out of bed wanting to do their best work because this is usually true, even when it might appear not to be. We've all had that 'difficult' person in the team who we assume wants to be difficult to spite us. Perhaps you are that so called 'difficult' person. Probably nobody told you that you are, but you sense it and make assumptions about what people think.

Whenever there is conflict, there is a tendency to assume that someone is deliberately trying to irritate. It's rarely the case. Most people are trying to do their best. Once we make assumptions, we act as though they are true.

Assumptions therefore make or break relationships. Pay attention to the assumptions you make. Positive ones can set expectations too high and cause people to fail. Negative ones can break down relationships and cause mistrust.

Judgemental assumptions

Assumptions are often made as judgements about people. One common assumption people make is that introverts don't have anything to say, or shy people are rude, or extroverts are self-absorbed. It's simply not true in most cases, but it's an example of how easy it is to make assumptions that are judgemental and cause distance in relationships.

Everyone will make assumptions and come to conclusions based on their values, beliefs and experience, and therefore everyone will make different assumptions about the same thing. Having an open conversation in the team will go a long way to breaking through the myths of assumptions. The more clarity you create by articulating assumptions, the easier it is to lead from the middle and align the team.

Negative self-talk or self-doubt is another form of assumption. If you assume you can't do something, you will behave as though it is true. Negative self-talk is a judgement on yourself. You judge yourself as not able, willing or capable. This will influence your decisions, actions and behaviours, and probably cause you to fail or prevent you from stretching out of your comfort zone. We will explore this more in the next chapter on intentions.

Often assumptions are projection. You may feel frustrated by someone who you deem to be standoffish. Explore how you show up as standoffish in that relationship too. In this way, we judge people based on behaviours that we are holding about them, and we behave as though our judgement is true and look for evidence to support it.

Above all, test out your assumptions without judgement. Assumptions are stories in your head. Change the story (assumption) to a more positive one and test it out with the other person.

Clarity is the antidote

Clarity is not only saying what you want to say. It involves having a common understanding about a situation or thing and working together as a team until everyone is on the same page. Most disagreements come about due to a lack of clarity and because assumptions have (often incorrectly) been made to bridge the gaps. If you don't understand something or you don't agree with something, be honest about it. Ask questions until everyone has a common understanding and assumptions are clarified. Whenever there is a lack of clarity, articulate what is known and also articulate what is not known so that there is a common understanding and assumptions are minimised.

In order to have clarity, be clear as a team on what you are trying to achieve. Have clarity on the overall goals and objectives, then break it down further so that you have a common understanding of the individual goals and objectives that make that up. Be clear what you are being asked to do.

Why is it important to you, to the team, the business, your customers, the world? What is the overall impact you are trying to create as a team and as a business? Is what you are doing the best way to achieve it? Creating clarity at every step will prevent the team making false assumptions and acting on them.

Be clear on the values, beliefs and behaviours within the team. Test your assumptions with each other, to prevent misunderstandings. Be clear what your expectations are from each other. If you feel frustrated with someone in the team, it's usually because there is a mismatch in what you want from them, what they think they should be doing, and what they might want from you.

Making time to be clear will resolve many disagreements within a team. Be clear on what your expectations are. Be clear on where you agree and where you disagree. Then build a plan to resolve the differences. Use the support of the wider team if two people disagree, and don't take sides. Support each other and have compassion for each other as you navigate this.

Don't confuse assumptions with facts. Use clarity to articulate the difference between hard facts, assumptions and emotions. Each of these is valid, and clarity can shine a spotlight on what is really happening. In the next chapter, we will explore how intentions help you align as a team and provide focus to achieve outcomes.

 If you'd like to explore this chapter with your own team, download the *OPUS Method of Team Performance* workbook from www.judejennison.com/opus and record your reflections and actions.

Chapter 15

INTENTIONS

In which we create a powerful impact through conscious action...

Setting an intention

The team was anxious. I felt their energy the moment they walked through the gate. I went into the field to bring the horses in to work with the team. Tiffin took off at a gallop, and the rest of the herd followed. My heart rate rose. I felt the brief anxiety of looking an idiot in front of the clients. I breathed slowly and slowed my heart rate down. As the horses came to a standstill, I approached them again. I felt a little unsure of whether they would cooperate or not. Once again, they took off, this time in response to my feelings of doubt.

I needed to set a clear intention. I knew that if Kalle came in, the rest of the herd would follow. I set an intention that Kalle would stand still for me to put her head collar on. I felt my energy shift as my thoughts and beliefs moved to more positive intentions. I walked calmly towards Kalle and stopped about five metres away. I said out loud: 'They are anxious. We are needed. Help me do this. I can't do it without you.' Kalle walked up to me and put her head in the head collar. The clients watched from the gate.

'What happened?' one of the clients asked. 'Is she the compliant one?' another client asked.

Kalle is far from compliant, but she sensed my intention and came willingly. When I am calm and clear, I can call on her to cooperate because she respects and trusts me. She may not understand my words, but she understands the energy of the intention behind them.

What are intentions?

An intention is defined in Wikipedia as 'a mental state that represents a commitment to carrying out an action or actions in the future. Intention involves mental activities such as planning and forethought.' We often use the word 'intention' when we are determined to achieve something. We set our mind to it and want it to happen. We tend to misuse the word 'intention' or the verb 'intend' when we talk about something in the future. *I intend to buy a farm this year*; *I intend to meet my sales target*; *I intend to have more time for self-care.* These are goals, not intentions. Often nothing changes, and you may or may not achieve what you wanted to. People often fail to meet their goals because they don't act with intention. Unless you shift your energy behind the intention, it becomes another word for want or wish or desire or goal.

So, what are intentions if they are not goals? Intentions are a state of focus and awareness. They influence how you show up. They don't automatically determine success, but they steer the course of where you go and how you get there. Intentions are more a state of being in the action of doing.

If you believe something won't work, it often doesn't. If you believe it will, it changes the energy with which you approach it. As a result, you act with more confidence and belief, and you give yourself a greater chance of success. I often say to clients: 'Whatever you do, lead wholeheartedly and decisively.' When there is uncertainty, as there often is, lead with confidence and conviction. This is a form of intention in itself.

We set intentions based on our beliefs, boundaries, assumptions, values and experience, as well as our vision and desires. We sometimes set them consciously and often set them unconsciously. Henry Ford famously said: 'Whether you think you can, or you think you can't – you're right.' As soon as you believe you can do something, your behaviour changes and there is a greater chance of success. Just as negative self-talk is a false assumption (as explored in Chapter 14), believing you can't do something also sets the intention for what happens next. Your actions are influenced by that false assumption.

An intention is based on a desire to influence behaviour overtly or covertly – your own or that of others. By having a clear and conscious intention, you influence your own behaviour, as opposed to meandering at will. You also influence others by providing clarity and the energy behind something intentionally.

Being intentional

Whatever you want to achieve, you create your reality by how you show up in any given moment through the beliefs you hold and the actions you take. Often, we take action unconsciously. If you don't think about the impact you want to create before you go into a meeting, how do you know if you will create a positive outcome?

Likewise, if you start a particular task that is difficult without a clear intention of making it easy, it is more likely to be challenging because that's the unconscious intention that you have set, and therefore the energy that you bring to the task.

Often if you believe a task to be difficult, it is because your energy reflects that belief. If you believe something to be easy and hold that as an intention, it is more likely that it will be because you shift your energy into being more relaxed and flowing.

Being intentional has determination, purpose, clarity and strength, about what you do and how you do it. There is no control, but there is a surety of focus. The purpose and strength of an intention need to be balanced by being relaxed, calm, assured, adaptable and flexible. Intentions are implemented from a state of flow, described by Mihaly Csikszentmihalyi (Csikszentmihalyi, 2002) as 'the state in which people are so involved in an activity that nothing else seems to matter' (p. 4).

Imagine a continuum from inaction at one end to control at the other. Somewhere in the middle is this state of 'flow'. This is the state from which you set intentions and create your reality purposefully. Paying attention to your body in any given moment enables you to shift your state to be more intentional and create the impact you want to create.

By raising awareness of your energy and emotions, you increase understanding of self, relationships and the field, enabling you to be more intentional about what action you take in the present moment, in order to achieve a positive result for everyone.

Collective intentions

The challenge for teams is that often people have different opinions about how things should be done. If you are to align as a team, you need to set collective intentions together. This might be a tacit intention, where there is a common understanding already within the team. Or it might require a team to discuss and agree what their collective intention is.

For example, if you ask three people to help you move a table from one place to another, there is likely to be a tacit intention that is shared by the group. You might provide instructions of what you want each person to do (leading from the front) but the intention is likely to be shared because the task is simple. Therefore, the chances of moving the table easily are high.

However, teams rarely just move things from one place to another! The world of work is much more complex and integrated.

In order for a team to have a collective intention, there are a number of factors that need to happen:

1. Each person needs to be clear on what is expected of them.
2. Each person needs to play their part.
3. Each person needs to believe the task is achievable and that everyone else will play their part.
4. Each person needs to believe that everyone also believes and is committed to playing their part.

You only need one person to lack focus or be out of alignment, and the collective intention can fall apart in a split second.

In the story at the beginning of Chapter 5, I describe an example of a team who tried to get Kalle to go with them to the gate and struggled. I recommend you re-read that example. It demonstrates how a lack of intention caused a team to lose focus on where they were going, and how they had multiple individual intentions, rather than a collective one. As soon as they had a collective intention and focus, Kalle joined the team and went willingly.

If one person doesn't do what they need to do for whatever reason, the others won't necessarily be able to make up for it. Therefore, collective team success is dependent upon a collective intention. When everyone plays their part in sync, you turn a collective intention into a reality.

No wonder teamwork is so difficult at times. By making Kalle a problem, the team had inadvertently judged her and put all their attention onto making her move. She wanted to be in a team who were synchronised, clear where they were going and believed in her playing her part. As soon as that happened, she demonstrated her personal intention of being willing to come with them.

The team could easily have judged her as unwilling, when in fact, she was very willing, but lacked clarity and alignment. You can see how easy it is to make assumptions when one person is not aligned. Instead, be curious about what they need and provide it. Most people are willing. If they don't cooperate, it's an opportunity to be curious about what you can do differently and how you can change your own behaviour. The non-verbal feedback is always more obvious if you turn your attention onto what you can do, rather than onto wanting everyone else to change.

The challenge of intentions

If your intention is different from the collective intention, it won't matter how hard everyone works, you'll be misaligned and pull in different directions. That's why it's important to resolve creative and practical differences and work collaboratively towards a common intention. Tension gets created whenever you are misaligned. If this happens, re-align using the Organisation

Model, set the clarity and direction and work together towards the same objective. Be intentional about doing this and how you do it.

It requires courage to act with intention, because often you only pay attention to needing to do so when you operate out of your comfort zone. This is easier for some than others; therefore, pay attention to the relationships and the stress levels within the team. What might be an appropriate intention for you might not be achievable for the collective. You may have to modify your expectations according to what is achievable with this team, in this moment, with the available resources, skills and time.

Setting too high expectations is common in teams and sets you up to fail. You can see how intentionally you create failure by being unrealistic in your intentions! Therefore, set intentions as a team, and be realistic about what is possible and what is not. Don't be afraid to call out unrealistic expectations.

Personal self-doubt can sabotage the whole team. If you don't think you can keep up, or achieve your part, you could derail the whole collective intention. Often people struggle on in the desire not to be the weak link. Instead, be clear about what is achievable and ask for help. It's a sign of strength to be vulnerable for the sake of the team success, and it's an act of courage to call out when something is not achievable, especially when the team is attached to a specific result.

Whenever frustration rises and someone loses their temper, the unconscious intention in that moment is to lash out at someone else, to wound and cause hurt, even though they may not have really intended it. Intention is not about being fixed and rigid in your thinking. There is a fluidity that is needed. Notice in your body how you hold tension when you become fixated. Notice the difference between moving intentionally towards a desired outcome, as opposed to being attached and trying to control the outcome.

When you set intentions, either individually or collectively, make sure that they are in service of the bigger picture. Does your intention meet your needs, the needs of the relationship(s), the needs of the team, as well as the market needs? For example, you can set an intention as a team to launch a product that the market does not want or need. This could lead to lack of sales in line with your projection or could lead to the market buying something it does not want or need. Manipulation is not the same as intention! Intentions should be in service of something greater than you and your team.

Making assumptions about who is committed to the team intention is common. Use open dialogue to prevent misunderstanding. Whenever you have a negative thought, whether towards yourself, others or a situation or thing, there is an opportunity to be clear on your boundaries, clarify your assumptions and be intentional in a positive way. The unconscious stories you tell can eat away at the team or can be an opportunity to reveal hidden dynamics that positively influence team performance.

 If you'd like to explore this chapter with your own team, download the *OPUS Method of Team Performance* workbook from www.judejennison.com/opus and record your reflections and actions.

Conclusion

CREATING THE MAGIC

In which we integrate the four steps and create the magic of team performance…

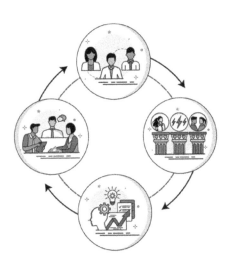

Chapter 16

REVEALING THE HIDDEN DYNAMICS OF TEAM PERFORMANCE

In which we overcome the challenges and lead the change…

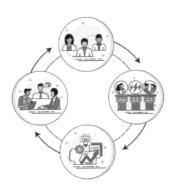

The stories we tell

'I don't like horses (or animals).'

'I went on a pony in Wales as a kid and the pony tanked off with me and I fell off. Dangerous beasts. I've never liked them since.'

'I went pony trekking as a child and my horse pulled into the grass verge and ate the grass. I couldn't get it to move. Everyone went off without me and I didn't know what to do.'

'My pony refused to move so they slapped it on the bottom, and it took off. I was terrified. I've never been near horses since. I don't like them.'

'My mother was bitten by a horse when she was holding me as a baby. She was terrified. I've never liked horses.'

I've lost count of how many times people tell me stories like this. They are great examples of introducing people to an experience for which they have no understanding and no skill and are set up to fail. Essentially, they are unsafe. As a result, they decide they don't like horses and never go near them again. Some may become terrified; others avoid the situation altogether (therefore avoiding even admitting the fear). Most people blame the pony. Some look at me and say: 'Perhaps it was me.' In reality, it's not the person or the pony. It's the relationship between the two and the context of the situation.

If you want people to learn, they need to feel safe to do so. Resistance in teams, and in learning, happens when people don't feel safe to explore. It takes courage to try something that you think you won't like or can't do, but this is the challenge of leading disruptive change.

Resistance to change

One of the most common questions I get asked is: 'How do I get people to do what I need them to do?' This puts people as a barrier to your success and is a major cause of stress. There is a subconscious desire to put the focus externally on changing everyone else, so you don't have to change yourself.

A better question is: 'What can I do to ensure my needs are met and achieve the team goals?' This shifts the responsibility back from external to internal. If someone doesn't do what you need them to do, there is a reason. Perhaps they need more clarity, more skill, more commitment. Whatever it is, be curious about what your needs are, what the needs of the other person are and work together to explore how you meet the team objectives.

'We both fear and seek change. Or, as one organizational consultant put it: "People don't resist change. They resist being changed"' (Senge, 2006, p. 144). Change is uncomfortable. It requires the humility to recognise that there is a different way of doing things than the way you've always done them. As teams gain in experience, they often become more closed to learning. They shut down experiences that have not worked before, even though it was in a different context with different relationships.

They might be willing to learn cognitively but nobody wants to admit that their emotions get in the way or their behaviour has a negative impact. Yet all of us have the ability to be brilliant and also to get in our own way, and therefore in the way of the team's optimum performance. Resistance to change is fear; fear of the uncertainty of how it might be done. In my book *Leading Through Uncertainty*, I explain:

> Resistance to change is often born out of the desire to hang on to what is known, understood and controllable... Resistance needs to be met with more space for curiosity and reflection. When you allow time for increased

169

observation and understanding, relationships grow stronger and minimise the divide.

(Jennison, 2018, p. 78)

There is a tendency to blame and judge resistance. Instead, consider it as a form of feedback. Give people space to work it out, to feel safe stretching into the zone of uncertainty, and take your time.

Team development takes care and skill, and the pace of everyone will be different.

Not enough time

And therein lies a problem. The problem of time. One of the biggest challenges facing teams today is that they are 'always on'. There is no time for reflection, no time to learn, no time to iron out differences of opinion. At least that's the popular view. I'd argue that you don't have time to avoid these things. An aligned team works much more quickly than a misaligned one who spend too long in lengthy debates, getting frustrated with each other's differences of opinion.

Imagine British tennis player Andy Murray saying he didn't have time to practise his serves because he was too busy playing games. He'd never get the aces he gets without the practice. This is true of business teams too. By reflecting on the non-verbal behaviours and taking time to practise new behaviours, performance is enhanced. This is a crucial part of every team member's role, although it is rarely given the priority it deserves. The time spent resolving differences of opinion and aligning together in the beginning will yield faster results later.

Whilst you are pushing through and getting stuck with the differences of opinion, another company is carving through because they have spent the time developing the team and therefore collaborate more quickly and effectively. Make time to enhance the team rapport and relationships.

You want a quick fix

There are no quick fixes with teamwork. It takes effort to build relationships. It takes courage and compassion to work through differences of opinion. It requires you to continually reflect on what you do and how you do it and explore different ways of inter-relating within the team. Finding your flow as a team takes commitment: commitment to the relationships in the team, to the objectives, to going the extra mile without burning out in the process. To know when to push through and when to draw back.

The desire for short-term fixes and results is a product of our time. It takes patience to work together as a team. When teams are under pressure, patience is often in short supply. Stress behaviour causes frustration when you don't get a quick result. There are no quick fixes when it comes to relationships.

Look at your family. There are patterns of behaviour that you repeat that don't work, disagreements that don't get resolved, assumptions made that are not necessarily true. There may be blame, judgement and criticism. A quick-fix approach to teamwork includes all of these. That's why spending time developing your team will improve the relationships, create more harmony and enable you to align and find your flow together.

Integrating the OPUS Method

The OPUS Method has been developed to help teams reveal the hidden dynamics of team performance. The four steps and 12 hidden dynamics may sabotage team success unless you reveal them and work with them consciously.

Let's explore how they work together here.

Step 1: The Organisation Model

In order to execute together, your team needs to align fully. It requires you to provide clarity from the front, to execute and communicate effectively in the middle and stay focused on the direction of travel, and to hold the team accountable (leading from the back). Keep raising awareness of how your team adopt these roles.

Whenever you are in flow, the three roles will be in play. Pay attention whenever there are challenges because one of the roles may need more awareness and focus.

Step 2: The Pillars of Vitality

Embrace the Pillars of Vitality. Minimise stress so that everyone works with maximum productivity. Whenever it is difficult, there is always another way. Find it. Use your individual and collective energy and emotions to support rather than derail the team, and to verbalise the non-verbal and create the quality of conversation that keeps you in sync and irons out differences of opinion.

Using energy, emotions and verbalising the non-verbal helps your team explore the three team roles in the Organisation Model. Whenever you are out of alignment, look for the energy and emotions that get in the way and create conscious conversations to resolve the differences.

Step 3: The Understanding Approach

The Understanding Approach provides additional information at times of uncertainty. Have the self-awareness to know whether you are in sync with the team and change your behaviour if you are not. Pay attention to your own wellbeing and energy and use it to influence the team positively. Notice which role you play in the Organisation Model and switch when something else is needed.

Continually sense into the relationships and make decisions based on what is happening and what is needed. Notice the Pillars of Vitality and the roles in the Organisation Model and evoke change in your own behaviour that positively influences others.

Focus as well on the wider field and the bigger picture so you see patterns unfolding, and pre-empt them using the Pillars of Vitality and roles in the Organisation Model.

Continually switching your awareness through all three levels of understanding provides additional information that might seem hidden but influences the team unconsciously. Make it conscious and have the quality of conversation that reveals the hidden dynamics and enables you to resolve issues easily before they escalate.

Step 4: The Stories Blueprint

The three unconscious stories enable you to work cohesively in the three roles of the Organisation Model. If you have unclear boundaries or constantly step over them, team cohesion is difficult. Having clear boundaries keeps you focused on the team intention. Having a clear intention as a team keeps you aligned.

By raising awareness of the unconscious stories, you improve wellbeing, using conversation as your route to reveal the hidden dynamics of the team.

Boundaries, assumptions and intentions guide actions and conversations, enable clarity of understanding and create more seamless execution when they are articulated.

The energy of intention is one of focus, determination, clarity and harmony. It is strong, yet relaxed. Clear, yet flexible. Determined, yet open-minded. There is always room for conversation, exploration and collaboration.

This is the challenge of teamwork, where everything is fluid, and the team needs to be present to whatever is emerging in any moment and respond accordingly. Together.

Continual learning

The hidden dynamics of team performance underlie every team. In the course of reading this book, you will see that they are not hidden at all. They unconsciously shape every relationship and action. By speaking openly about hidden dynamics, you enhance what is already working and do it more, as well as explore where you sabotage your success. Success lies in the continual learning of who you need to be in any given moment.

Change is never easy, especially when it involves years of conditioned behaviour, individually and collectively. But if you got this far in the book, it's because you know there is something else that is possible for you as a team. The desire to resolve differences, to create harmony, to work in a state of flow, to do work that makes a difference in your business and in the world. This is what is possible for you and your team.

You can't do it alone. Changing your behaviour will have an impact and make a difference to the team, but in the end it's a team effort. Effort spent on the team communication and relationships will increase efficiency and productivity. It will reduce stress and tension in the team. You'll sleep better at night, instead of worrying about who is doing what and how you get them to do what you want them to do.

Create the dream team. It starts with you all, as a collective.

Summary

I hope you have experienced the magic of brilliant teamwork in your working life. It is a source of great joy to work completely in flow, in alignment with others, building on the strengths of each other, working collaboratively together, resolving differences of opinion with humility, having the courage and compassion to engage in the difficult conversations, being clear on where you are going together and knowing that everyone is committed both to each other and to the end goal.

This is the magic of brilliant teamwork. It's effortless. It's flowing. It's joyful. Sadly, it's rarely that easy. Along the way, there are disagreements, differences of opinion to resolve, challenges to overcome, relationships that break and need rebuilding, trust that needs to be upheld and effective communication under pressure. Invest the time, energy and emotional effort and you make it easier to resolve differences of opinion.

It's no secret that you are doing great work. Lift back the covers and reveal the hidden dynamics of the team. Therein lies the gold of team performance. Do it together, with honesty and transparency. Together, you can achieve anything. The world needs you.

 If you'd like to explore the hidden dynamics with your own team, download the *OPUS Method of Team Performance* workbook from www.judejennison.com/opus and record your reflections and actions.

THE LIFE AND DEATH OF TEAMWORK

Figure 6: Opus
© Copyright John Cleary Photography 2019

I was mentally and emotionally prepared for this day but physically unprepared when it happened. I arrived at the stables in a dress and heels, dressed for client meetings in the city, not for what I was about to do in a field of mud in the pouring rain. When Opus saw me, he perked up and rushed to get to me, even though walking was difficult for him. I wrapped my arms around his neck and told him he was safe and could trust me. The day I had been dreading had arrived. I was ready for what I had to do and who I needed to be.

Opus completely surrendered and leaned his weight into my shoulder, something he'd never done before. The other side of the fence line, only three metres away, the rest of my herd of horses stood watching. My yard manager stepped back to give us space. He had my back, and I felt reassured by his presence. I was working with the herd, following their every move, as they followed mine. Breathing in and out as one, emotionally and energetically connected. Working in harmony, knowing that what we were doing was life changing for everybody and life ending for one of us.

Opus knew it too. He leaned on me further. I promised him that I loved him, that he was safe and that I would look after the rest of the herd. He completely trusted me in that moment in a way he had never done before. As he took his last breath, he fell to the ground, and I felt an utter sense of peace. It felt as though the world had stopped. The sheer silence as everyone stood still, still breathing as one. I was unaware of being soaked to the skin by the continuing rain, still in my dress and a pair of wellies I'd found at the stables. The herd followed my every move and every breath, and I followed theirs; we trusted our instincts and our teamwork in every moment. Co-creating together. Leading through uncertainty at a time when it mattered most.

I opened the fence line to allow the herd to come and see Opus and say their goodbyes. The rain continued to pour. As I knelt by his head on the ground, I looked at Kalle, my lead mare, and said to her, as if to reassure her: 'He's gone, darling. He's gone.'

Kalle looked on in horror, her head held high in fear, as if she were trying to make sense of what was happening. She had relied on Opus for strength and confidence for seven years, as had I. She scuttled towards us, gave a massive snort and took off at a flat-out gallop around the field, her mane and tail flying behind her. She galloped three times around the field with the rest of the herd following her, as if she were doing laps in his honour. They were majestic. The herd pulled up, panting, and stood snorting at a distance. I still knelt at Opus's head, stroking his face, telling the herd it was ok, he was at peace and not to be scared. One by one they came forward, touched him and stood around his body, honouring him.

Suddenly aware that I was getting cold in the rain now, I stood up and took a step back. I sensed this was a moment for the horses to pay their respects, and I was now in the way. As I stepped back, a flock of geese appeared as if from nowhere and flew silently over Opus's body into the distance. I've never seen them before or since. I've since read that geese often appear at funerals.

As an inter-species team, we had followed our instincts and led from each other. Each one trusting in the others. I have never felt so safely held as I was that day by the herd. I have also never before been trusted the way Opus and the rest of the herd trusted me in that moment, watching me and looking to me for leadership, even though I had no idea what I was doing.

This is the magic of brilliant teamwork, using the hidden dynamics of the team to perform together as one, right to the last breath.

MEET THE EQUINE TEAM

Every business needs a high-performing team, and I'm grateful to have handpicked mine. All of my horses are rescue horses. They have been retired from riding careers for various reasons. None of them can now be ridden, so they come to me to do a new job. Here is the Leaders by Nature team.

Kalle

Kalle is a black 16.2 hands Trakehner mare, born in April 2000. Trakehners are a German breed and a mix of Arab and thoroughbred breeding. Trakehners are highly sensitive, and often horse riders describe them as tricky. In fact, I find them to be very straightforward and extremely suitable for my work. They want to work in partnership, and they don't like to be told what to do. It makes them ideal for this work because they need you to balance absolute clarity and direction with a strong relationship, and to invite them to work with you, not for you. If you listen to them and pay attention to their needs, they are very willing. If you try to dominate them or push them around, it's a disaster!

Kalle was my first horse and started this work in January 2012. She is highly intuitive, and she knows which buttons to press to give you great learning. She has a massive range and brings whatever is needed to give clients the best learning. She knows when to challenge and when to back off and be gentle. She switches from one end of her leadership range to the other in an instant.

She has a self-assured presence that people often find intimidating. Many people avoid her at the beginning of the day, thinking she will be challenging. In fact, she is extremely gentle and kind, and as long as you blend clarity, direction and relationship in equal measure, she willingly follows you anywhere. Learning from her is guaranteed.

Kalle is the leader of the herd so when she moves, everyone else follows. It is a privilege to work and learn with her.

Figure 7: Kalle
© Copyright John Cleary Photography 2017

Opus

Opus came to me in July 2012, aged 24 when he retired from his riding career. He was a 16.1 hands dark brown thoroughbred. He was a descendant of a horse called Northern Dancer, the highest-earning racehorse of all time. Opus was born in Australia in 1988 and lived in New Zealand, Bahrain and then the UK, so he was well travelled and the most experienced of the herd in terms of riding experiences. He competed in just about everything with his owner Laura.

Opus was challenging with CEOs, MDs, executive teams and senior leaders because he expected them to lead without dominance. With graduates, he was gentle and easy, so they went away with more confidence. Opus took charge unless you matched his alpha male presence. Whereas Kalle requires a softer energy, Opus required a strong, masculine energy in order for him to pay attention. However, if you raised your energy too much, you could easily enter a power struggle with him. Opus demanded that you find that knife-edge of assertiveness in order for him to come with you.

Figure 8: Opus
© Copyright John Cleary Photography 2017

Opus had the free run of the yard and was the welcoming party to clients, sometimes not letting them through the gate! He would stand outside my office, watching every sales meeting I ever had, and regularly demand hobnobs, his favourite biscuit.

Opus would decide who he wanted to work with. He would kick the gate and demand to be let in to work with someone. He would march up to a chosen person, head butt them as if to say 'You, work with me.' It was a privilege for clients to be chosen by him. He missed nothing, and I always knew he had my back.

Opus passed away in August 2019. He continues to have an impact on clients through the stories we tell about him.

Tiffin

Tiffin was the third horse to join me in June 2014 at the age of 13. He is a dark bay 16.3 hands Irish thoroughbred and was born in Ireland in April 2001. He raced in Ireland and was brought to England to hunt. He was sold every year for four consecutive years. The last place he lived was a riding school where he was treated with kindness, possibly for the first time in his life.

Having been sold repeatedly, and his home never being quite right for him, I was Tiffin's last chance at life – a responsibility I take very seriously. When Tiffin arrived, he looked older than his years. His face was misshapen, and I thought he had taken a tumble during his racing or hunting days to cause this. Over time, as he has relaxed into his home, his face is gentler, he looks younger, and I realise that his misshapen face was the tension of stress and anxiety.

Tiffin connects deeply with those who have physical or emotional challenges. He will often connect with the person who is emotion-ally struggling, or he will touch injured parts of the body with his nose. His demonstrates empathy by the bucket load. He recently walked with a limp with a client who had a plate in her leg!

Tiffin has become more playful as he relaxes and is often the one to instigate a boxing match with the young boys, inviting them to rise up on their hind legs and play with him. Tiffin is deep and highly sensitive. He has difficulty trusting people, but if you trust him absolutely, he will join you in that place.

Figure 9: Tiffin
© John Cleary Photography 2017

Mr Blue

Mr Blue arrived in October 2015, aged only five years. He is a 16.2 grey Trakehner gelding. He had arthritis by the age of five, which meant he was severely lame on arrival. He was still a very young horse who had no idea where his feet were and often stumbled over them and made us laugh.

Mr Blue loves people and is highly interactive. He is the class clown and likes to goof around. He pushes the boundaries and took the longest to integrate into the herd because he didn't pay attention to herd behaviour. He invades personal space repeatedly and likes to pick up your feet with his teeth. If you let him, he pushes the boundaries further, and has been known to steal hats and gloves from clients!

Mr Blue provides a lot of the humour and fun on workshop days. He loves toys and is easily distracted, so he causes teams to get derailed on a regular basis unless they are extremely focused, clear and work as a cohesive unit.

Mr Blue reminds us not to take life so seriously and to make leadership fun. He also shows how to balance playfulness without losing respect or focus. Often clients who get easily distracted or love to play have a hard time with him because he takes advantage of them. Mr Blue teaches clients the balance of how to use your energy appropriately.

Figure 10: Mr Blue
© Copyright John Cleary Photography 2017

Gio

Gio joined the Leaders by Nature team in June 2017 at the age of seven. He was Mr Blue's half-brother, although they looked very different. He was a 17.2 hands black Trakehner gelding who was never ridden due to ongoing lameness. He had the sweetest personality, and this was his first job.

Although Gio was the largest of the herd, he was the gentlest, and he connected on a deep level. He liked to nuzzle your ear and breathe into your nose. He was the first to look up when you entered the field and often the first horse to come over. He was interested in all clients and loved the work. He created a heart-to-heart connection that had to be felt to be understood. He was often the one that clients wanted to take home at the end of the day.

Figure 11: Gio
© Copyright John Cleary Photography 2019

The master of compassion, Gio had such a massive heart, and in his presence, you could feel your own heart expanding as you stood with him. Gio passed away suddenly in November 2019, aged nine years. Adored by everyone, Gio was a gentle giant and is missed terribly.

Admiral

The newest, and youngest, of my team, Admiral was born in 2012. He joined the team in November 2019, a week after Gio's death. He is Mr Blue's (and Gio's) half-brother, all sharing the same Trakehner father. His mother is a breed called Holsteiner, a large carthorse breed. Admiral is the tallest of the herd, standing at 17.3 hands high. He was injured in the field when he was two years old so has never been ridden. As a result, he has the least life experience of all of my horses and is a bit like a gentle but clumsy foal in a large body.

Figure 12: Admiral
© Copyright John Cleary Photography 2020

The first time I went to pick his feet up, he shook me off so hard, I nearly went through the fence. He looked surprised at how physically strong he is and how weak I am in comparison! He is learning to be gentler with us and is willing and curious about the work with clients. He works well with clients when loose in the field and is often the first horse to come over and meet someone new. He is less sure of himself in the arena in more controlled exercises and can be anxious when led with a head collar, typically because clients are anxious leading him, and he picks up on their insecurity.

Admiral requires a lot of clarity, confidence and direction, just as an inexperienced member of a human team would who is new to their job. He is still finding his feet and his confidence is growing.

GRATITUDE

Thousands of people have influenced me over the years, and I am grateful for everything I've learned around a topic that is so embodied for me that I struggled to put words to it.

I am forever grateful to the following:

The thousands of IBM colleagues from all over the world who I worked with over 17 years – you were some of the smartest, most heart-centred people I've ever met.

My beta readers, Anne Archer, Inger Bowcock and Mark Pinches: your generous and courageous feedback caused a major re-write of most of this book. Thank you. We're all grateful for that!

My research students, Zoe Barron and Francesca Jordan: your extensive research provided new insights, substantiated my ideas and saved me hours of time.

My accountability group, Rebecca Mander, John Cleary and Steve Hooper: you kept me focused and sane through the laughs, the tears, the goals achieved and the highs and lows of 2020.

Laura Savage: thank you for trusting me with Opus. I think he'd be proud of how well he taught us both.

My publisher, Alison Jones: you are an all-round amazing human being who makes teamwork effortless. Your unwavering belief in me kept me going.

My friend and mentor, Alan: I value your support and cherish your friendship. You energise and stretch me. I've achieved more, knowing you always have my back.

My horses: Kalle for headbutting me when I'm not present, Opus for listening, Tiffin for showing me what I'm doing wrong and demanding better leadership, Mr Blue for making me laugh, Gio for expanding my heart and showing me the gift of sadness, and Admiral for reminding me that I can, and do, embody everything in this book.

Paul, you never wanted pets but somehow agreed to a total of five cats, two dogs who bred 60 puppies between them, six horses and counting in our 30 years of marriage. Here's to many more (animals as well as years of marriage)! Thanks for giving me freedom to express myself fully and authentically in life and work. I promise to keep failing and learning.

ABOUT JUDE JENNISON

Jude Jennison is an award-winning executive team coach, author and speaker, specialising in leading fast-paced change. A business owner since 2010, Jude previously worked for IBM for 17 years, where she managed a budget of $1 billion and led UK, European and global teams.

Jude develops the leadership skills of executive teams and entrepreneurs to accelerate business results through greater clarity, connection and commitment. She works with a herd of horses to uncover the default patterns of non-verbal communication that enable teams to be more effective. She has coached over 3,000 leaders and teams.

Jude is an international speaker on leadership matters and author of the books *Leadership Beyond Measure* and *Leading Through Uncertainty*.

Jude has been featured on BBC Two and BBC Radio 4, as well as being featured in the *FT*, Virgin Entrepreneur and local radio and press. She is a regular writer for *HR Director* magazine.

Jude is the Founder of Leaders by Nature and the creator of LeadershipAcademy.Online. She is cited in the Thinkers 360 list for Top 100 Global Thought Leaders and Influencers you should follow in 2021.

She hosts three leadership podcasts which you can find on her website and two of her podcasts are featured in the Thinkers 360 Top 50 Business Podcasts to listen to in 2021.

- Leading Through Uncertainty
- Rethinking Leadership
- Innovating Humanity

Contact Jude

JUDE JENNISON
LEADERSHIP WITH A DIFFERENCE   www.judejennison.com

jude@judejennison.com

judejennison

jude.jennison

leadersbynature

judejennison

BIBLIOGRAPHY

Banholzer, M. M. (2019). Fielding high-performing innovation teams. Retrieved from McKinsey & Company: www.mckinsey.com/business-functions/strategy-and-corporate-finance/our-insights/fielding-high-performing-innovation-teams

BITC. (2019). *Mental Health at Work 2019: Time To Take Ownership.* Retrieved from: https://www.bitc.org.uk/report/mental-health-at-work-2019-time-to-take-ownership/

Bugental, J. F. (1990). *Intimate Journeys.* Jossey-Bass.

Collins, A. et al. (2019, January). *The Global Risks Report 2019.* Retrieved from World Economic Forum: www.weforum.org/reports/the-global-risks-report-2019

Csikszentmihalyi, M. (2002). *Flow: The Psychology of Happiness.* Rider.

Ekman, D. P. (2018, January 5). The benefits of emotional awareness. Retrieved from Psychology Today: www.psychologytoday.com/us/blog/between-cultures/201801/the-benefits-emotional-awareness

Finzi, B., Lipton, M., Lu, K. and Firth, V. (2020, July 9). Emotional fortitude: The inner work of the CEO. Retrieved from Deloitte: www2.deloitte.com/us/en/insights/topics/leadership/ceo-decision-making-emotional-fortitude.html

Fogel, A. (2013). *Body Sense: The Science and Practice of Embodied Self-Awareness*. W. W. Norton.

Gendlin, E. (2003). *Focusing*. Rider.

Hofmann, L. (2014). Brief introduction to existential psychology. Retrieved from YouTube: www.youtube.com/watch?v=oyTzv7V1kvA

Hunt, V. L. (2015). *Why Diversity Matters*. Retrieved from McKinsey and Company: www.mckinsey.com/~/media/McKinsey/Business%20 Functions/Organization/Our%20Insights/Why%20diversity%20 matters/Why%20diversity%20matters.pdf

Jennison, J. (2015). *Leadership Beyond Measure*. CreateSpace.

Jennison, J. (2018). *Leading Through Uncertainty: Emotional Resilience and Human Connection in a Performance-driven World*. Practical Inspiration Publishing.

Moyers, B. (1989). *A World of Ideas: Conversations with Thoughtful Men and Women about American Life Today and the Ideas Shaping Our Future*. Doubleday Books.

Obama, M. (2018). *Becoming*. Viking.

Paperback Oxford English Dictionary (2012). Seventh edition. Oxford University Press.

Pang, A. (2018). *Rest*. Penguin.

Scharmer, O. and Kaufer, K. (2013). *Leading from the Emerging Future*. Berrett-Koehler Publishers Inc.

Senge, P. (2006). *The Fifth Discipline: The Art and Practice of the Learning Organization*. Random House Business Books.

Siegel, S. H. (2017, October). *Mental Health and Wellbeing in Employment: A Supporting Study for the Independent Review*. Retrieved from Deloitte: www2.deloitte.com/uk/en/pages/public-sector/articles/mental-health-employers-review.html

Sinek, S. (2014). Twitter post. Retrieved from https://twitter.com/simonsinek/status/431448539739463680?lang=en

Stevenson, D. F. (2017). *Thriving at Work: The Stevenson / Farmer Review of Mental Health and Employers*. Retrieved from https://assets.publishing.service.gov.uk/government/uploads/system/uploads/attachment_data/file/658145/thriving-at-work-stevenson-farmer-review.pdf

Taylor, F. (2017). *Relational Leadership: When Relationships Collide with Transactions (Practical Tools for Every Leader)*. High Bridge Books.

Vickberg, S. P. (2019, June). *The Practical Magic of 'Thank You': How Your People Want to Be Recognized, for What, and By Whom*. Retrieved from Deloitte: www2.deloitte.com/us/en/pages/about-deloitte/articles/time-to-rethink-employee-recognition-strategy.html

Wheatley, M. (2002, April). It's an interconnected world, *Shambala Sun*. Retrieved from Margaret Wheatley: https://margaretwheatley.com/wp-content/uploads/2014/12/Its-An-Interconnected-World.pdf

Wheatley, M. J. (2010). *Perseverance*. Berrett-Koehler Publishers.

Wheatley, M. J. (2017). *Who Do We Choose to Be?* Berrett-Koehler Publishers.

Yalom, I. D. (1980). *Existential Psychotherapy*. Basic Books.